THE
UNITED STATES
AND THE
SOVIET UNION

A Background Book on the Struggle for Power

By ROBERT A. LISTON

Parents' Magazine Press
New York

Each Background Book is concerned with the broad spectrum of people, places, and events affecting the national and international scene. Written simply and clearly, the books in the series will engage the minds and interests of people living in a world of great change.

To R. MacG. N.C. and Sally

Library of Congress Cataloging in Publication Data

Liston, Robert A
    The United States and the Soviet Union. New York,
Parents' magazine Press, [c1973].
    (Background book)
    Bibliography: p. 284p.
    1. United States—Foreign relations—Russia.
2. Russia—Foreign relations—United States.
3. United States—Foreign opinion, Russian.   4. Russia
—Foreign opinion, American.   I. Title.
E183.8.R9L58   327.73′047   72–10553
ISBN 0–8193–0678–9
ISBN 0–8193–0679–7 (lib bdg.)

CONTENTS

ACKNOWLEDGMENTS

The author is indebted to Miss Connie Jenkins, a senior student, and Miss Thelma Bumbaugh, librarian, at his alma mater, Hiram College in Ohio, for making books available to him. The staff at the Westport Public Library, Westport, Connecticut, was quite helpful. Special appreciation goes to Mrs. Eleanor R. Seagraves of Washington, D. C., who found many useful items for him.

Both author and publisher are grateful for permission to quote from a number of books, as follows:

Nations in Darkness: China, Russia and America by John G. Stoessinger. Copyright © 1971 by Random House, Inc., New York. Reprinted by permission of the publisher.

Soviet Politics At Home and Abroad by Frederick L. Schuman, Alfred A. Knopf, New York, 1946.

America and Russia in the Changing World by W. Averell Harriman. Copyright © 1970, 1971 by W. Averell Harriman. Reprinted by permission of Doubleday & Company, Inc.

The Last 100 Days by John Toland, Random House, New York, 1965, 1966.

The Rivals: America and Russia Since World War II by Adam B. Ulam. Copyright © 1971 by Adam B. Ulam. Reprinted by permission of The Viking Press, Inc.

Present At the Creation: My Years in the State Department, by Dean Acheson. Copyright © 1969 by Dean Acheson. By permission of W. W. Norton & Company, Inc.

Intervention and Revolution by Richard J. Barnet. Copyright © 1968 by Richard J. Barnet. Reprinted by arrangement with The New American Library, Inc., New York, N.Y.

A New Foreign Policy for the United States by Hans J. Morgenthau, Praeger Publishers, Inc., New York. Coypright © 1969 by the Council on Foreign Relations, Inc.

Cold War and Counterrevolution by Richard J. Walton. Copyright © 1972 by Richard J. Walton. Reprinted by permission of The Viking Press, Inc.

Specific pages on which these quotations appear are indicated in the *Notes,* beginning on page 262.

1

ANTI-COMMUNISM CHALLENGED

It's understandable that the Russian economy has progressed so fast in such a short period of time. I mean, after all, they haven't had to spend half of their money fighting communism.

— **Jim Teter** *and* **Jim McDonald**

THE TWO MEN quoted are a young American comedy team. They listed the above as among their favorite jokes in the July 8, 1972 issue of *Parade* magazine, a Sunday supplement.

The joke commences this book, not because it is to be a frivolous one, but because jokes often are very serious. Humor has long been studied by scholars as a barometer of changing public attitudes. Comedians frequently relieve the tensions of people by giving ex-

1

pressions to their feelings. Satirizing governmental policies is as old as man.

Two comments may be made about the Teter–Mc-
Donald joke. First, its daring is a bit surprising. The
joke probably could not have been uttered at all ten
years ago and would not have been very funny five
years ago. Fighting communism was so much a part of
our national policy a decade and more ago, we were so
dedicated to the concept of giving our national all to
containing the Red menace that one simply did not
crack jokes about it.

Second, and more important, the existence of the
witticism in a mass-circulation magazine probably indicates a fundamental change in American attitudes
toward communism and Soviet-American relations.
There is a common, perhaps prevailing, opinion in the
United States today that:

(a) our immense investment in lives, money, and
national energy in fighting communism has not been
successful, advantageous, or necessary;

(b) whatever wisdom our opposition to communism
may once have had, it is now intellectually and morally bankrupt;

(c) new attitudes and policies must be adopted; and

(d) both communism and democracy have come full
circle and are more alike than dissimilar; in short the
ties that bind them are stronger than the ideologies
that separate them.

It is probably impossible to compute the cost of our

opposition to communism. The Korean War from 1950 to 1953 alone cost the United States 33,629 battle deaths and 20,617 non-battle deaths, plus the wounding of 103,284 men. The Vietnam War, the longest and most difficult in our history, had cost more than 45,000 American lives in combat with more than 150,000 hospitalized from wounds at the time this was written.

The killing and maiming in these two wars may well be the least of the bloodshed in the name of anti-communism, if anyone could compute the total figure. Any full account must include the lives and injuries in such places as Laos, Thailand, Cambodia, Dominican Republic, Cuba, Guatemala, Lebanon, and other places where American military might has been used or its use threatened in the twenty-five years from 1947 to 1972. The list must include our spies, most of them unknown or unrecognized, who were shot or imprisoned by Communist nations. The largest figure of all will be those soldiers, sailors, and airmen whose lives were lost in accidents in the line of duty—the lost planes, the sunken ships—through the training and maintenance of a multi-million-man military force which America has long believed it needs to oppose and contain communism.

Not to be forgotten is the disruption in the lives of the millions of men drafted for the military services since World War II, and their families.

The monetary cost, again not computed, must run into the trillions of dollars. In the eleven years from

1960 through 1970 alone, the United States spent $664 billion for defense and defense-related industries.[1] The United States maintained in 1971, according to a congressional investigative committee, "some 375 major foreign military bases and 3,000 minor military facilities spread all over the world . . ." [2]

We have expended vast sums for foreign military and economic aid, partly for humanitarian purposes, but mostly to prevent those nations from going Communist or to help them oppose Communist insurgencies. The House Committee on Foreign Affairs computed that the United States appropriated over $90 billion from 1948 through 1971 for military and economic foreign aid.[3] In 1971, President Richard M. Nixon told the nation that over $142 billion had been spent on foreign aid in the quarter century after World War II.

Our national intelligence or spy apparatus currently costs in excess of $5 billion a year. When the costs of the White House, congressional committees, the State Department, and more than thirty other agencies[4] involved in war or foreign operations are included, the direct and indirect cost of our anti-communism comes to a total beyond comprehension.

There is a reverse cost associated with the money spent in fighting communism. The money spent on armaments, spying, and foreign aid was not available to be spent at home for domestic purposes. Our serious urban problems—such as blighted housing, inferior education, submarginal mass transit, crime, drug addiction—are a product of monetary neglect, as are such national problems as pollution, racial tensions, strikes by underpaid civil servants, prisons that breed criminals, court reform, and many others. Such problems cannot be blamed on communism or anti-communism, but certain it is that the federal government would have been able to spend more money on alleviating these problems had not so much of our national budget gone for defense against communism.

There is another result not too indirect to be mentioned here. The war in Vietnam, in particular, has spawned dissent, demonstrations, riots, and bloodshed. The nation's long commitment to anti-communism has led in the last few years to vocal opposition to that policy, to national disunity, disrespect, diminished patriotism, and a national disagreement over our goals and morality.

We will go into these matters in more detail in pages to come, but at this point some other direct costs of our "crusade for freedom" should be mentioned. Attorney General A. Mitchell Palmer engaged in an out-and-out anti-Communist pogrom during World War I and Senator Joseph McCarthy led a thoroughgoing Communist witchhunt following World War II. Large numbers of scholars, public officials, writers, military officers, and just plain citizens were faced with contempt and ill-repute in the name of anti-communism. Dissent was silenced. Study of communism was diminished. Loyalty oaths were required. To this day, some Americans have sought on many occasions to throw away our most cherished civil liberties in the name of anti-communism. The Fifth Amend.nent to the Constitution (part of the Bill of Rights), granting freedom from self-incrimination, was made in the not-very-distant past an object of scorn and incrimination by insinuation. We have had political trials upon political trials. We have sought to silence dissent by labeling it Communist, when that dissent had not the faintest relationship to Moscow or Peking.

In foreign relations, we have supported, in the name of anti-communism, some most unsavory dictatorships because they happened to be avowedly anti-Communist or said they were. We have supported these dictatorships even when they were suppressing, sometimes by brutal means, the legitimate aspirations of their people for the freedoms we enjoy and were supposedly defending. We have thereby seen our international reputation besmirched. We have become in many places in the world "Mr. Moneybags" at best and a source of repression at worst.

Perhaps most serious of all, we have undergone, through anti-communism, significant changes in our form of government. The military may not have become dominant in the federal government, but generals and admirals have today a far greater say in spending, national priorities, and diplomacy than ever before in our history. We have in America a highly uncharacteristic secrecy in government, with "top secret" and "secret" labels being attached routinely to material, at least some of which bears only the slightest relationship to national security. Even Congress, to say nothing of the public, has great difficulty discovering what is happening in our nation's three-million-member bureaucracy.

We have witnessed since World War II a vast growth in the powers of the president at the expense of Congress and the people. As the nation's commander in chief and chief diplomat, a succession of presidents have conducted the nation's foreign affairs—which has meant largely anti-communism—as a personal exercise leading to the bloodshed and vast expense. Congress, the judiciary, and the people have found no direct way to stay the presidential hand in foreign affairs. He is largely free to do as he sees best, then explain later in the most favorable light what he has done. Such changes in our historic system of government may be right, necessary, and inevitable. But certain it is that our opposition to communism has been a major factor in their occurrence.

To sum up, we may safely say that the United States has paid a high, high, high price for its opposition to the Soviet Union and its Communist ideology.

What is disturbing (if the Teter–McDonald joke has validity) is not that we paid the high price, but that the most apparent result of it all challenges the wisdom of what we did. The Soviet Union has not grown weak but strong. The issue no longer is whether the United States is militarily *more* powerful than the USSR but whether we are as strong in nuclear, missile, naval, air, and army weapons. The Soviet Union has not surpassed the United States in economic strength, but is apparently sufficiently strong for its purposes and growing stronger every year.

Our postwar policies may have saved Western Europe from communism, but some of those nations, notably France, are not especially fond of us today. The South Koreans, whom we defended at great cost, announced, in 1972, a program of rapprochement with the North Koreans with unification as the goal.

We have lived for more than a decade with the avowedly Communist and most unfriendly nation of Cuba located ninety miles off our shores. Nothing remarkably terrible has happened in that time. The government of Chile, long one of our staunchest friends, went Communist by an elective process. Again, nothing very untoward happened and the United States accepted it with as much grace as possible.

Such dubious nations as South Vietnam, Laos, Thailand, and Cambodia remain in existence in Southeast Asia largely because of American battle casualties and billions of dollars in American aid. The North Vietnamese and insurgents in other countries seem to receive adequate amounts of Russian and Chinese aid to stay in business and thwart our best efforts. Indeed, North Vietnam, surely one of the weakest nations on earth, seems able to survive the worst we can do to it militarily and then ask for more.

For nearly a quarter of a century we supported the former government of China, the Nationalist government under Chiang Kai-shek. In the meantime, our staunchest allies, such as Britain, France, and Canada, recognized the Communist People's Republic in China. We can do nothing about it. Ultimately, we joined in the vote to admit the People's Republic to the United Nations, but were defeated in our efforts to prevent the ejection of Nationalist China from the organization.

The East Germans and Russians built a wall in Berlin to separate the eastern part of the city from the west. We condemned it, but now live with it. The peoples of Hungary, Poland, and Czechoslovakia, hungry for liberty, rebelled. They were enslaved by Russian tanks. We sat by helplessly.

We witness cultural exchanges of ballerinas and other artists, applaud exchanges of scientific information, and look forward to joint American-Russian space efforts. Trade with the Soviets, which not long ago was denounced as anti-American, is now being actively sought.

The results most apparent to Americans involve the journeys of President Nixon to Peking and Moscow. Mr. Nixon began his political career as a militant anti-Communist. He campaigned and was elected in 1968 as a moderately conservative president. Yet, in 1972 he was shown on television from Peking drinking toasts in "strong rice wine" with a score of Chinese Reds who not long before had been considered America's enemies. After his visit to Moscow, he tossed off his fatigue and hastened to the Capitol to address a joint session of Congress to explain that the arms limitation and other agreements he had signed were in no way a sign of American military weakness or a diminution of American commitment to national defense.

Clearly, after all these years of lives lost, money spent, and turmoil in the name of anti-communism, we have seen the enemy grow strong and have learned to live with communism in the world. Most of our best international friends, notably Britain and the Western European democracies, practice forms of state ownership. American industrialists such as Douglas Grymes, president of the Koppers Company, are urging Americans to admit "the truth . . . that free enterprise has indeed disappeared" in America, admit that ours is a planned economy and, having admitted it, engage in more and better planning as the Japanese, West Germans, and other Western European countries do—not to mention the Russians.

We have social security, unemployment compensation, medicare, poverty programs, aid to education, and a hundred other social programs—and clamor for still more. The United States government spends one-tenth of all the money expended in the United States and there are many who would have it spend still more. The president and his advisors are expected to plan and manage the economy to prevent unemployment, low production, and hard times. If that planned economy necessitates wage and price controls, such as President Nixon invoked in 1971, that is generally approved.

The point has become obvious to large numbers of Americans that our historical opposition to communism no longer quite squares with the way the world is nor with the economic, social, and political aspirations of Americans at home.

Some questions are raised. They have been asked and answered for many years by scholars. They are being asked by older people who grew up and lived for a quarter century under our militant anti-communism. Most certainly they are being asked by young people who never knew the rationale for the anti-Communist crusade or who question its validity for today. Children who have lived through the futility of the war in Vietnam, they legitimately ask what the evil is in communism and why we have opposed it so.

Some of the questions are these: Why are we so against communism? Why do we hate the Russians, distrust them so, and feel compelled to oppose them so consistently? Has this opposition been wise? Have we paid too high a price for too little gain? What might we have done differently that would have achieved a better result at a lower cost? More importantly, how can we change our reflex anti-communism? What should our new policies be in the world that exists today? Can we be friends with the Russians and Chinese and other Communist peoples and stop the arms race, war, and waste?

Before seeking answers, we must pose these questions: what are the origins of our anti-communism? Why did we hate it enough to make all those sacrifices? In short, how did the past half century happen? We must search our history and try to discover what events and attitudes in the past led to the tragic consequences and the long-standing impasse.

There are three ways to view this history. The prevalent view in America is that the fault for the cold war lies mostly with the Russians. They were imperialistic, grasping, bent on ideological if not actual domination of the world, unreasonable, intransigent. The United States, while it made some errors, had no real choice but to combat the Communist menace and seek to contain it. We should be applauded for our sacrifice and courage.

The second view in America is that proffered by the so-called revisionist historians. Much of the fault is America's. Admittedly the Russians were difficult following World War II. They were bent on carving out a sphere of influence in Eastern Europe. But we Americans were naïve and unrealistically idealistic. We failed to understand the Russian motives and to try to ameliorate Russian fears. We embarked on a tough policy of opposition and containment and thrust the world into two rival camps. There were many opportunities for settling the cold war, or at least for reducing tensions, but blind to reality we failed to follow up on them.

The third view of Soviet-American history is probably the most accurate. It was set forth by Professor John G. Stoessinger in his well-received book *Nations in Darkness*.[5] He saw the Soviet-American conflict as rooted in the imperceptions the leaders of each nation had of the other. The Russian Communists and the Americans possessed an unreal view of each other which was based on their unreal conceptions of themselves. The Soviets saw America through the film of Marxist doctrine. Americans saw the Soviets through their conception of freedom and democracy. Thus, in Professor Stoessinger's opinion, neither side saw the other correctly. The mutual misunderstanding of motives and aims resulted in mistrust and impasse.

Not only does Stoessinger's view of Soviet-American history appear to be most accurate, but it also seems to offer the most hope for the future.[6] If we can understand the fraudulent views each side has had of the other and the unfortunate actions that have resulted from them, then perhaps these imperceptions can be straightened out and amicable relations established in the future.

2

AMERICA AND THE RUSSIAN REVOLUTION

THE RUSSIAN REVOLUTION occurred in 1917. By 1972, the United States had experienced fifty-five years of almost unrelenting hostility to that revolution and the Communist party which assumed power as a result of it. In 1972, the United States was not yet two hundred years old as a republic. Thus, for more than a quarter of our existence as a nation we have given ourselves over to a virulent antipathy to communism. They have been perhaps our best years, when we had the money and know-how to make America a paradise. That we have invested (some would say squandered) at least some of that money and know-how in fighting communism cannot be doubted.

Some strange anomalies have occurred in those fifty-five years. Twice in that period we fought Germany;

Italy and Japan once. The wars against those peoples took far more lives (400,000 in World War II) and called for greater sacrifices than any of our efforts against Communists. Yet West Germany, Italy, and Japan are today among our closest friends and staunchest allies. Except for one brief intervention in 1919–20, Americans have never fought the Russians directly. They were, in fact, allied with us during World War II against Nazi Germany and Italy. Yet we forgave the Germans and accepted them as our allies in our hostility to the Russians. The issue is not that such an action was wrong or bad. The issue is that our action was passing strange. We ought to pursue the reasons for our hostility to communism.

Moreover, we had not liked what the Communists revolted against in 1917. The Russian tsars were an American symbol for despotism. Theirs was considered autocratic rule, the antithesis of democracy, something left over from the distant past. When, in the early 1900s, George F. Kennan exposed the tortures and other inhumanities of the tsarist slave labor camps in Siberia, Americans considered the Russian rulers unspeakable. Indeed, one of the criticisms Americans made of the British and French, with whom our sympathies lay in the war against Germany that began in 1914, was that they were allied with the Russians.

There were two revolutions in Russia in 1917, the so-called February Revolution and the October Revolution. So decadent was tsarist Russia that it was still using the old Julian calendar which was by that time two weeks later than the Gregorian calendar used in the rest of the world. Thus the February Revolution occurred in what the rest of the world considered March and the October Revolution in November.

The first revolution deposed Tsar Nicholas II and created the so-called Provisional government under Prince Lvov and later under Alexander Kerensky. American foreign policy approved of this revolution and sought to keep its leaders in power, Russia in the war, and the nation a secure place for American investments. We wholeheartedly opposed the Bolsheviks who threatened to overthrow the Provisional government, take Russia out of the war, and seize all foreign property.

America greeted the first revolution with enthusiasm. The despotic tsar had been evicted. Democracy had triumphed. President Woodrow Wilson expressed the American attitude in April 1917, in his speech to Congress asking for a declaration of war against Germany.

Does not every American feel that assurance has been added to our hope for the future peace of the world by the wonderful and heartening things that have been happening within the last few weeks in Russia? Russia was known by those who knew it best to have been always in fact democratic at heart, in all the vital habits of her thought, in all the intimate relationships of her people that spoke their natural instinct, their habitual attitude toward life. The autocracy that crowned the summit of her political structure, long as it had stood and terrible as was the reality of its power, was not in fact Russian in origin, character, or purpose; and now it has been shaken off and the great, generous Russian people have been added in all their naïve majesty and might to the forces that are fighting for freedom in the world, for justice, and for peace. Here is a fit partner for a league of honor.[1]

America's almost total misperception of Russia, the Russians, and what was going on there is set forth in that statement. As George F. Kennan, one of America's diplomatic experts on the Soviet Union, put it:

> I need scarcely remind you that practically every element in this moving statement [the Wilson speech quoted above]—the belief in the democratic tradition and instincts of the Russian people, the belief that the Tsar's government had been an alien regime, the belief that the common people of Russia saw the war (rather than internal revolution) as a means whereby freedom, justice, and peace were to be attained—reflected a complete misunderstanding of the real situation in Russia. The statement did honor to Wilson's generous ideals, not to his knowledge of the outside world.[2]

America's relations with the Provisional government of Russia might be considered a comedy of errors had it not been so tragic. The story has been told in detail by historian William Appleman Williams.[3] It is too long a tale to tell here, but we can list some of the more unfortunate American mistakes.

American diplomatic personnel in Russia in 1917 were, with one major exception, both inept and blind to what was going on. Our ambassador was David R. Francis, a St. Louis grain dealer. On the ship to Russia to assume his diplomatic post in 1916, he began an affair with an attractive German woman who was widely believed to have been a German agent. For months, he refused all entreaties from his staff in Moscow and from the State Department in Washington to break off the affair. He consistently sent back glowing reports of the prospects for the success of the Provisional government, when in fact its chances of remaining in power were bleak.

In June 1917, Wilson sent over an investigative commission headed by Elihu Root, a former secretary of state and conservative corporation lawyer. He, too, completely misread what was going on in Russia. His most famous statement on the trip was uttered while touring a Siberian village: "I am a firm believer in democracy, but I do not like filth." [4]

The person most aware of what was happening in Russia in the summer and fall of 1917 was Raymond Robins, an American labor leader who was part of the American Red Cross mission in the Russian capital. His analyses of the Russian situation were ignored or disputed.

Robins understood at the time and historians now

agree that the Communist party, particularly its Bolshevik faction, were the real power in Russia all during the days of the Provisional government. The Bolsheviks had deliberately refused to assume power in the February Revolution, feeling they were not yet strong enough to rule the country. They were husbanding their strength and giving the provisional rulers rope on which to hang themselves.

In his efforts to have grain distributed to the starving Russian people, Robins discovered that he had to deal with local Communist Party Soviets or party councils. These Soviets distrusted him as an American capitalist, but he was on many occasions able to break down the distrust and obtain grain. Through these and other contacts with the people, Robins came to understand the plight of the Russians, their longing for peace, and their determination to complete the revolution and institute a government of the masses. At the very least, the Communist party was the best organized by far in Russia. In many parts of the country it was the only organization.

In Washington, the American ostrich put its head in the sand. The Wilson administration was motivated by two policies. It wanted to protect the sizeable American investments in Russia, as well as provide opportunity to increase them. The leading figure in this was banker J. Pierpont Morgan, who controlled, or sought to, most of the American loans to Russia or to American companies in Russia. Morgan directly or indirectly supplied most of the leading experts on Russian affairs in the Wilson administration.

More importantly, Wilson wanted to keep Russia in the war against Germany. The Russians were not doing much fighting on the eastern front and what they did was done very poorly, but at least they were tying up many German troops. If Russia left the war, those troops would be freed to possibly overwhelm the English, French, and American troops on the western front. Our entire diplomatic effort went into keeping the Russians in the war, but this unfortunately was done mostly by persuasion by Ambassador Francis and Elihu Root. According to historian Williams, Wilson and his secretary of state saw the Root mission as "one primarily designed to 'show our interest and sympathy.' Faced with unpleasant reality [Bolshevik power], Wilson and his advisors practiced self-deception. They were to find that easy road built on quicksand." [5]

There was perhaps no way for the Provisional government to survive against the Bolsheviks. But what chance it had, men such as Robins consistently warned, depended upon peace and bread. The Russian people wanted to be out of the war and they wanted food, and this is precisely what the Bolsheviks promised to bring them. If the Americans, English, and French had permitted Prince Lvov or Kerensky to end the war or had offered massive foreign aid of food and other necessities, it is reasonable to suppose that the Provisional government might have remained in power. At one point

William Boyce Thompson of the Red Cross mission spent a million dollars of his own money to supply needed commodities to the Russian people.

Instead of peace and bread, the American, English, and French governments urged that a major offensive be launched on the eastern front. "We are tossed about like debris on a stormy sea," said Prince Lvov,[6] but the offensive was launched with disastrous results. Lvov was forced out of office and Kerensky installed in July 1917.

The situation steadily worsened during the summer of 1917, until even Ambassador Francis had to admit conditions were in "a very unsatisfactory shape" and "growing more grave all the time." [7] Americans sought a scapegoat and found him in Vladimir Ilich Lenin, leader of the Bolsheviks.

Unwilling to believe that Lenin and his number two man, Leon Trotsky, headed a popular revolution, Americans decided they must be German agents. Since Germany was America's enemy, it was natural, perhaps inevitable, that all the world's troubles be blamed on the Germans. This theory was supported by the fact that Lenin had hidden from tsarist police in Germany and had been transported back to Russia in a sealed train at the start of the revolution. But Lenin was not a German agent. The Germans were perfectly willing to make use of him if he could subvert Russia and take it out of the war, but they were not paying him or telling him what to do.

Thus, from the outset of the Russian Revolution in February 1917, Americans were beset by a whole gaggle of misconceptions about what was happening. Stoessinger uses the term "psycho-logic" to describe the phenomenon. We believed what we wanted to believe, not the reality of what was happening. Ambassador Francis saw only the success of the Provisional government because he wanted it to be successful. Root saw only dirt, Wilson only democracy, Morgan only money to be made, because that is what all of them wanted to see.

When the Bolsheviks assumed power in October 1917, American misconceptions only deepened. They believed the Russian people, democratic at heart, had had their wonderful democracy under Kerensky stolen from them by a gang of German agents led by Lenin and Trotsky. It would be only a matter of time, thought Americans, until the democratic spirit of the Russian people would assert itself and throw out the Red rascals. Stoessinger gives an appealing statement of such fraudulent views in *Nations in Darkness*:

> When the Bolsheviks seized power in November 1917, most Americans reacted as if the impossible had happened. And since it was impossible, it would soon cease happening. Again, a distinction was drawn in the American mind between the Russian people and the "usurping gang" of Bolshevik leaders. The American missionary spirit asserted itself in the pages of the influential New York *World*: "Russia cannot be abandoned, either to Germany or to anarchy."

The predominant belief in the United States was that the Bolsheviks were a small minority whose crazy ideas would soon topple them from power, whereupon the democratic instinct of the Russian people would again rise to the surface. The New York *Times,* according to a study made by Walter Lippmann during the period from November 1917 to November 1919, predicted the fall of the Bolsheviks from power no fewer than ninety-one times. It also reported four times that Lenin and Trotsky were planning flight and three times that they had already fled. Three times it announced Lenin's imprisonment and once even his death.[8]

The German agent theory was given a boost when the Bolsheviks signed a separate peace treaty with the Germans at Brest-Litovsk in March 1918. Incredibly the idea lingered on for some years after Germany surrendered to the Allies in November 1918, and there was no point in their having agents any more.

The notion that the Bolsheviks were a minority who imposed their will on the democratic masses by force or subterfuge was a long time in dying. There are still Americans who believe it today. The belief that communism would soon disappear was a major factor in the American intervention in Siberia in 1919–20. President Wilson, after some hesitation, sent nine thousand American troops to join with British, French, and Japanese contingents to aid White (as opposed to Red) Russian forces in their effort to unseat the Bolsheviks by force of arms. At one point the White Russian and foreign troops controlled most of the country. But the Bolsheviks enlisted the support of the people and the Red Army won the civil war. It is widely believed that the foreign troops, rather than defeating the Bolsheviks, aided them. The Russian people had a patriotic reaction to the invasion and rallied to defend their own country.

The intervention offered the Bolsheviks another advantage aside from unifying the nation. They were able to use it for decades to propagandize their people. It was used as evidence of the imperialism of capitalist countries and of their fear and hatred of the Soviet Union. The evilness of the invaders and the heroism of the defenders became greatly magnified through propaganda. As late as 1957, *Pravda,* the Russian newspaper, reported in connection with the fortieth anniversary of the Russian Revolution:

> In an effort to throttle the young republic of the Soviets, the imperialists, led by the leading circles of England, the U. S. A., and France, organized military campaigns against our country. From all sides—from north and south, east and west—the attacking hordes of interventionists and White Guards poured into our territory. . . . For over three years the Soviet Republic was obliged to fight off the mad armed attack of the combined forces of the imperialist beasts of prey. . . .[9]

When armed intervention failed to topple the Reds from power, the United States lapsed into a policy of non-recognition which continued until 1933. The So-viet Union, the largest nation on earth, was relegated to the status of non-person. It was the work of the devil and civilized people did not truck with the devil. This again was related to America's belief that the Bolshe-viks were a minority who had seized power only tempo-rarily. If America ignored them, perhaps they would go away.

All the while a massive, perhaps unparalleled hate campaign against Bolsheviks and communism was be-ing waged throughout the United States, in the White House, Congress, press, and pulpit. President Wilson said "the new dictatorship in Russia was just as selfish, ruthless, and pitiless as that of the Czars, and his heart went out to the ill-starred masses." [10] The Soviets were variously termed beasts, godless, the enemies of civilization. America stood for all that was good, free, and civilized in the world. Russia under the Soviets was the epitome of evil, slavery, and brutality.

This hate campaign required more fuel than just the Bolsheviks, who were after all a long distance away. Reds had to be found at home to be hated and they soon were. In 1917 Congress passed the Espionage Act, giving the government the right to censor newspapers, ban publications from the mails, and prosecute anyone who interfered with the draft or enlistment of soldiers. Conviction bore a punishment of up to twenty years in prison and a ten-thousand-dollar fine. This act, along with the companion Sedition Act of 1918, are considered as infamous in American history as the Alien and Sedition Acts in the John Adams administration.

The acts were the legal basis for the Red scare activities of Attorney General A. Mitchell Palmer. Historian Samuel Eliot Morison calls Palmer "a Pennsylvania politician with a Presidential bee in his bonnet." [11] Palmer fanned the flames of hate against Reds, radicals, and just about anyone who was in dissent. On a single night in January 1920, Palmer's agents arrested more than four thousand alleged Communists in thirty-three different cities. In Detroit, three hundred were arrested on false charges, held for a week in jail and denied food for twenty-four hours, later to be found innocent of any involvement in revolutionary movements. In New England, hundreds of people who had no connection with any sort of radical movement were arrested in another series of raids.

Deportation proceedings were begun against 5,000 "Red" aliens. Send them back to Russia was the cry. Fortunately, saner heads in the Wilson administration managed to have the deportation proceedings conducted in a legal manner with the accused permitted defense counsels and a fair hearing. Even with these precautions, more than 600 aliens were deported. On December 21, 1919, 249 persons were put aboard the *Soviet Ark* to Russia. One of Palmer's supporters said, "My motto for the Reds is S. O. S.—ship or shoot. I believe we should place them all on a ship of stone, with sails of lead, and their first stopping place should be hell." [12]

The hate campaign made a mockery of America's Bill of Rights. In New York, the state legislature expelled five Socialist members, although the Socialist party was legal in the state and the members were innocent of any offense.

Then in June 1921 came the Sacco-Vanzetti case, one of the most celebrated political trials in American history. Nicola Sacco was a shoe cutter by trade, Bartolomeo Vanzetti a fish peddler. Both were anarchists active in the labor movement. On May 5, 1920, in the midst of the Red scare, they were arrested and questioned about their radical activities. The following day they were charged with the murder of a paymaster and a guard during a payroll robbery near Boston. Vanzetti was also charged with another attempted holdup.

The trials of Sacco and Vanzetti were a mockery of American justice. At the first trial of Vanzetti, Judge Webster Thayer told the jury, "This man, although he may have not actually committed the crime attributed to him is nevertheless morally culpable, because he is the enemy of our existing institutions." [13] Evidence at the murder trial was inconclusive at best. Witnesses for the prosecution testified they had seen Sacco and Vanzetti at the scene of the crime. The defense produced other witnesses who had seen them miles away when the murders were committed. Yet Judge Thayer, who again presided, told the jury that Sacco and Vanzetti were either "conscious of guilt as murderers or as slackers and radicals." He appealed for a conviction, urging the jurors to remember "the American soldier boy . . . giving up his life on the battlefields of France" [14] in World War I.

The two men were convicted. Appeals dragged through the courts for six years until they were executed in August 1927. The case became a *cause célèbre* around the world. There were many demonstrations and strikes, and when Sacco and Vanzetti were executed, a quarter of a million people marched silently through the streets of Boston. The trials were denounced at the time and for years afterward by America's outstanding lawyers and judges.

Attorney General Palmer had nothing directly to do with the Sacco-Vanzetti case. He was no longer in office by that time. But indirectly, through his Red scare techniques and massive, illegal arrests, he was a major factor. He made the country see Reds where few if any existed. A form of national hysteria about communism was the result.

Palmer had another effect. His Red-baiting tactics made him an instant celebrity. He became a household word in America and won the support of large numbers of Americans. It very nearly won him the White House. Palmer believed he would get the Democratic nomination in 1920. But he and William G. McAdoo, who was Wilson's son-in-law and secretary of the treasury, fought each other to a standstill at the Democratic

National Convention. To break the deadlock, Governor James A. Cox of Ohio was named, along with Franklin D. Roosevelt as his running mate. Both lost by a landslide to Republicans Warren G. Harding and Calvin Coolidge.

Yet Palmer had come close to the nomination. The effectiveness of Red-baiting as a stepping stone to political power was not lost on the next generation of politicians in America. As we shall see, it became a habit.

Why did we fear and hate communism so? What was there about it that could lead us to sacrifice our most cherished liberties to combat its influences? Why would we take up arms against it? Why did we refuse to recognize the Soviet government?

These are important questions. To seek answers we are going to have to look at what communism was and what the Bolsheviks did. This will not only perhaps illuminate the origins of our hate, but of equal importance show the sources and nature of the Soviet imperception of America.

3

WHY WE HATE
COMMUNISM

WHAT IS COMMUNISM? What is all the shouting—and
dying—about?

The safest thing to say about it is that it doesn't exist
on any significant scale anywhere in the world, most
especially in the Soviet Union, which practices *state
socialism,* something else entirely.

Communism is a utopian political-economic scheme
for a society of angels. Under communism, everyone
would know what to do, enjoy doing it, and go about
doing it. He would receive wages or goods or services
in accordance with his needs. There would be no government (state) simply because it would be unnecessary. Every one of the angels would have full freedom
to spread his goodness before his fellowman. The most
plentiful commodity would be love.

It is probable that the United States has had more experience with communism than the Russians. The Christian religion has always sought a society of angels, if not on this earth, then in heaven. Brotherly love, understanding, mutual helpfulness, charity have long been American goals as well as those of other nationalities. They may not have been practiced as much as Americans think, but far more than critics believe.

Perhaps more than any other nation, America has founded utopian societies based on Communist principles. When we had the frontier, it was relatively easy for groups of like-minded people to buy or appropriate some land, set up a community and try to live like angels. There were the Shakers, Owenism at New Lanark, the Phalanx best typified at Brook Farm, the Oneida Community, the Mormons. We are still at it today with the so-called hippie communes, in which bands of people try to live together in peace, harmony, and brotherly love.

Communism is only an ideal and, as an ideal, who can fight it? It probably embodies the aspirations of man—at least some of the time. It is an ideal in the Soviet Union. According to Lenin and every Communist leader since, the state will eventually wither away and the glorious day of communism will arrive. Unfortunately, the Soviets have been at it fifty-five years thus far and have made no observable progress toward the goal.

What the Russians do have—they call it an interim

state leading to communism—is socialism. This is another economic system in which the means of production (factories, farms, machinery, tools, etc.) are owned by the government or state, which represents the people. Gone are the stockholders, the private owners, the coupon clippers. Workers are employed by the government and the profits from their labors are utilized for the benefit of the workers or the people.

Socialism, as an economic system, has a long history of turmoil. Capitalism, which is a system of private ownership of the means of production, fought government ownership or socialism for a century. We still do or at least talk about doing it in the United States. But opposition to socialism has become rather meaningless by now. Probably every nation on earth practices some forms of socialism today, including the United States. The federal, state, and local governments own billions of dollars' worth of factories, power plants, dams, forests, farms, and transit facilities which are operated for the public benefit and at minimum profit. We don't attach the word socialism to it, but nonetheless that's what it is.

Our closest allies in Western Europe, including the Scandinavian countries, France, Italy, and England, are avowedly Socialist. The major industries, including railroads, airlines, steel, and auto are owned wholly or in large measure by the governments of their respective nations. Western Europe collectively, under socialism, is considered both economically powerful and democratically sound.

Western Europe and other nations throughout the world are said to practice democratic socialism. This means that politically the nations have free elections and operate as democratic republics, much as the United States does. It also means that governmental control of the industry it owns is relatively loose. Managers of the steel, auto, or other industries are permitted to run these companies as they see fit to make them productive and efficient. There are few decrees from the central governments telling managers what to do and how to go about it. Only the stockholders have been replaced under this form of socialism, which is to say the private owners receiving profits. Moreover, under democratic socialism not all means of production are state-owned. It does not extend to farms, stores, small businesses. Only the major, vital industries are state-owned. And one of the characteristics of these is that they don't operate very differently from the privately owned corporations in America.

Obviously, there is considerable room for variance in the amount of industry owned by the state and the amount of planning and regulation it imposes. Among the Western European nations, Britain has less state ownership and regulation than some of the Scandinavian nations.

One of the identifying features of the so-called Communist nations is that they have a high degree of state ownership and regulation. In the Soviet Union, nearly all the means of production are owned by the state, including factories, farms, businesses, stores, machinery, and equipment. About the only important exceptions are the small plots of ground owned by the Russian farmers. They may grow small crops for their own needs and sell some excess to the public.

The Russians and other Communist nations (again there are variances) impose a high level of regulation. The Soviet Union has an immense, some would say stifling, bureaucracy of state employees who supervise and regulate nearly everything—production, wages, prices, goals, expenditures, and much more. It is still socialism, but because of the high degree of government control, it is termed state socialism.

Two other characteristics differentiate the allegedly Communist nations from the Socialist. The USSR, China, and other Communist nations avow that communism is their ultimate aim. Second, they are politically undemocratic. There is little or no political opposition. Freedom of expression, assembly, and religion are sharply curtailed. They are totalitarian dictatorships.

As a political system, totalitarian dictatorships do not have to be economically Socialist. Indeed, many are not. Nazi Germany and Fascist Italy, although they used the term Socialist in describing their form of government, were almost entirely capitalistic. Fascist Spain today, although it has some public ownership of railroads, bus lines, and similar industries, is largely capitalistic.

All this does not contribute very much to understanding why Americans have consistently hated communism and Communists, nor what the peculiar perception of the Soviets was that led them to misunderstand America and its intentions. It does help us to understand that Americans could dislike communism because it is totalitarian, but that does not explain why we could ally ourselves with a totalitarian nation such as Spain just because it is anti-Communist.

The bone in the American throat is the economic theory of Karl Marx, the intellectual father of communism, the Moses, Jesus, Mohammed, and Buddha of Communist ideology.

Karl Marx was born in Germany in 1813 and lived until 1883. He spent most of his productive years in England where he witnessed and experienced most of the suffering of the workers. He was a first-class scholar and thinker, but not a money-maker. He lived largely on the largesse of his co-worker, Friedrich Engels. His poverty led to the death of several of his children.

Seeing and experiencing the horrors of industrialization in England, Marx developed his theories. In the simplest terms, he proffered an economic view of history. A specific class of people could rule only so long as it represented the economically productive forces of society. When it became outmoded and unproductive, it would be replaced. In this manner, the bourgeois (capitalist) class had replaced the unproductive feudal nobility and effected the industrial revolution. In Marx's view, the stage was now set for another and final change. Having accumulated the factories, equipment, and other means of production, the capitalist class was no longer economically useful. Workers (the proletariat) were the productive members of society, and they would displace the capitalist class and seize control of the means of production.

In an advanced industrial nation, workers could not help but realize that the value of the goods they produced was far higher than the wages they were paid, the difference going into the pockets of the capitalist class. It was inevitable, Marx believed, that the workers would unite and seize power from the capitalists through revolution. The proletariat would become the ruling class, centralize all means of production under the state, and rapidly increase productive forces. Class distinctions would gradually disappear or "wither away" because, amid economic plenty, class antagonisms would gradually cease. Such bourgeois institutions as the family and religion, which had been used to perpetuate bourgeois domination, would vanish and each individual would find his personal fulfillment.

To militant anti-Communists in America, even today, Marx is considered a bearded, egghead, crackpot theoretician of dubious practicality and probably venal motives. The simple truth is that Karl Marx was an important scholar and thinker of the mid-nineteenth century. His economic view of history has had immense influence. He is the source for Communist ideology. Socialism was greatly influenced by him, although its exponents came to believe the workers could assume power through evolution rather than revolution. He had, if only negatively, great influence on the development of capitalism itself.

Most non-Communist economists feel that Marx made a mistake in his theory. Living in England in the midst of the industrial revolution and seeing the suffering of the workers, he was unaware of the concept that the suffering represented economic savings. (At least some of the money *not* paid to workers as wages went for more plants and equipment.) Nor could he predict that the fledgling social reform movement in England (and the United States) would eventually prevail to end child labor, long hours, low pay, and unsafe working conditions. He could not foresee that workers would unite, not to form national governments, but to force specific improvements in wages and working conditions or that capitalism itself would change to embrace greater distribution of wealth through higher wages, social changes, and government spending. But such a criticism of Marx's theory embodies a great deal of hindsight. The question is whether those changes would have occurred naturally or whether they were forced because of the appeal Marxist thought had for workers.

What is important to this discussion is that Marx's ideas are used to explain the mistakes of capitalism and the virtues of communism. He is all things to his believers.

The trouble was that the USSR—or the East European nations, or China, or North Korea, or North Vietnam, or Cuba or anywhere else communism is practiced—was not exactly what Marx, or Lenin for that matter, had in mind. For a proletarian revolution to sweep aside the bourgeoisie and topple a corrupt capitalist government, the nation had to be in an advanced stage of capitalism in which the rich were getting richer and ever more useless and the workers were being exceedingly oppressed. Britain, France, Germany, perhaps the United States seemed ideal for such a revolution. Russia of 1917 was hardly worth considering.

Russia was a huge land with a corrupt and despotic rule under the tsars, but it was only in the early stages of capitalism. The Russian workers were surely oppressed, but there weren't very many of them. Russia was a largely agricultural nation with many millions of oppressed peasants, and Marx had not had much to say about peasants. Put another way, Russia was still a significantly feudal society. Under Marxist theory, the capitalist class had not yet had much of a chance to overthrow the useless feudal class. But Russia is where the world's first proletarian revolution occurred, and Lenin rushed there on his secret, sealed train to make the best of it.

Perhaps the unsatisfactoriness of Russia as a locale for the revolution was the cause, but for whatever reason, Lenin, Trotsky, and other Bolshevik leaders, despite the problems of fomenting the Russian Revolution, seizing power, and fighting off foreign troops, found time to encourage world revolution. In fact, they considered world revolution essential to the success of the Bolshevik Revolution in Russia. Twelve days after the abdication of the tsar, the Petrograd (now Leningrad) Soviet issued a "Proclamation to the Peoples of the World":

> Comrade proletarians and all laboring peoples of all countries: . . . The time has come to start a decisive struggle against the intentions of conquest on the part of the governments of all countries. . . . We are appealing to our brother-proletarians of the Austro-German coalition and first of all to the German proletariat. . . . Throw off the yoke of your semi-autocratic rule in the same way that the Russian people shook off the Tsar's autocracy; refuse to serve as an instrument of conquest and violence in the hands of kings, landowners and bankers, and by coordinated effort we will stop the horrible butchery which is disgracing humanity and is beclouding the great days of the birth of Russian freedom. Laboring peoples of all countries: we are stretching out our hands to you in a brotherly fashion over the mountains of corpses of our brothers, across rivers of innocent blood and tears, over the smoking ruins of cities and villages, over the wreckage of the treasures of culture. We appeal to you for the reestablishing and strengthening of international unity. That will be the security for our future victories and the complete liberation of humanity. Proletarians of all countries, unite! [1]

Soon after the October Revolution, *Pravda* published this:

> The army of the Russian Revolution derives its strength from countless reserves. The oppressed nations of Asia—China, India, Persia—are just as eager for the fall of the regime of capitalistic oppression as are the oppressed proletarian masses of Europe. To fuse these forces in a world revolution against the imperialistic bourgeoisie is the historical mission of the Workers' and Peasants' Russia. The flame of the Petrograd revolution will inevitably grow into a fiery hurricane that will strike to the ground the sword of this piratic war and turn the dominion of capital to ashes.[2]

In statement after statement, the Bolsheviks indicated that their major goal was world revolution. In 1917, the Soviets quite incredibly appropriated two million rubles to help foment revolutions outside Russia. In 1918, the Soviet constitution repudiated all past debts as a first blow at "international financial capitalism" and promised to continue the effort until the "international revolt of the workers against the yoke of capitalism shall have secured a complete victory." By 1919, Nikolai Bukharin, a leading Bolshevik, was saying the "Communist revolution can triumph only as a world revolution. . . . The Communist working class movement can win only as an international Communist movement."[3]

Export of revolution was not very successful following World War I. There was a short-lived Communist revolution under Bela Kun in Hungary and an attempted one in the Bavarian section of Germany, but both were overpowered by foreign troops.

Lenin, Trotsky, and their successor, Joseph Stalin, did not discard the notion that the workers of the world would unite, rise up, and smite down capitalism through revolution. They held to this belief despite the fact that it did not happen and despite overwhelming indications that it probably would never happen.

Whatever hopes there might have been for world-wide Communist revolution were dashed in the 1930s when the entire capitalist world was mired in a deep and long-lasting depression. When workers still did not rise to revolution, despite the unemployment and poverty, the possibility of its ever occurring were remote. The workers of the world did unite, largely within national borders, yet those labor unions consistently rebuffed both communism and Communists. American workers struck, fought, and died in battles against industrial corporations, but they never seriously considered revolution. Their battles were for specific demands for higher pay and better working conditions.

In Western Europe, workers were more politically active, forming Socialist parties and vying for government control. But again, both by design and in practice, the change from capitalism to socialism occurred peacefully with little that resembled political or economic revolution.

Through it all, the Soviets held to the Marxist notion that the workers of the world would rise in revolt. Like the American idea that the Bolsheviks were German agents soon to be thrown out by the democratic Russian people, the Communist notion of world revolution died slowly and hard.

The Soviet leaders steadfastly held to a fraudulent perception of the United States and other capitalist countries. The result was a view of the rest of the world garishly colored by Communist ideology.

Lenin knew very little about the United States except that it was capitalistic and thereby destined to be destroyed by a proletarian revolution. Trotsky had more acquaintance. He had lived in New York from January 13 to March 27, 1917. He had resided in a rooming house in a working class district on East 162nd Street, worked in the editorial offices of a Russian language Socialist newspaper, *Novy Mir,* studied American economic life at the New York Public Library, and practiced "his only profession," that of revolutionary socialist.

Ten weeks or so in any land is not long enough to get acquainted with it, but Trotsky seems to have been remarkably deficient in learning much at all. Shortly after the October Revolution, Trotsky told a Bolshevik meeting why the United States entered World War I.

It was the first direct utterance by any Soviet leader relative to the United States:

> The United States began to intervene in the war after three years, under the influence of the sober calculations of the American Stock Exchange. America could not tolerate the victory of one coalition over the other. America is interested in the weakening of both coalitions and in the consolidation of the hegemony of American capital. Apart from that, American war industry is interested in the war. During the war American exports have more than doubled and have reached a figure not reached by any other capitalist state. Exports go almost entirely to the Allied countries. When in January Germany came out for unrestricted U-boat warfare, all railway stations and harbors in the United States were overloaded with the output of the war industries. Transport was disorganized and New York witnessed food riots such as we ourselves have never seen here. The finance capitalists sent an ultimatum to Wilson: to secure the sale of the output of the war industries within the country. Wilson accepted the ultimatum, and hence the preparations for war and war itself.[4]

How much of this did Trotsky believe? The world may never know how much was deliberate propaganda on his part and how much he honestly believed to be true. It may perhaps be said, however, that Trotsky believed *some* of this to be true, such was his capacity for self-deception.

Lenin was not only a slavish follower of Marxist doctrine. He was an original thinker. Since his death in 1924, he has been lionized by each successive generation of Soviet Communists. His embalmed body is displayed in a glass casket in Red Square in Moscow. His every written word and utterance has the character of gospel. Indeed, Foy D. Kohler, former United States Ambassador to the Soviet Union, has stated that the Russians revere Lenin more than Marx.

> I have been trying to remember whether I ever heard a Soviet official or Soviet citizen quote Marx to me. I can't think of a single instance. But Lenin—yes: "As Lenin said . . ." "As Lenin taught us . . ." And nine times out of ten the quote which follows is one you feel sure would make Marx turn over in his grave.[5]

One of Lenin's main contributions to Communist ideology was his theory (stated as fact) that capitalist nations, reaching an advanced state of decadence, turned imperialistic. He developed the idea in *Imperialism, The Highest Stage of Capitalism,* which he wrote in exile in 1916. England, Germany, and Japan had already reached this stage. Their empires were proof of that and World War I was further proof, with the great imperialistic powers bent on destroying each other in their mad thirst for land, markets, and money. Lenin wrote that the United States, whose economic expansion had been "even more rapid than in Germany and for this reason the parasitic features of

American capitalism stood out with particular force," [6] would soon clash with other capitalistic, imperialistic powers.

Lenin and Trotsky utterly disbelieved Wilson's statement that the United States entered the war to "make the world safe for democracy." Lenin considered America just as imperialistic as Germany and determined to go to the "same savage and insensate lengths" to attain its ends. Needless to say, from Lenin's point of view, only a revolution of the proletariat would save America from itself.

It is also safe to say that the American intervention in the Russian civil war only intensified Lenin's conviction and his hatred for America. We may also assume that Lenin's notion of imperialistic capitalism remains a cardinal principle of Communist ideology. To this day, Communist propaganda from Moscow and Peking rings with the adjective "imperialist" to which such nouns as "dogs" and "beasts" are attached in descriptions of Americans.

In 1960, following a summit meeting of world Communist parties, a communiqué defined an independent national democratic state. It said in part:

> A state that consistently defends its political and economic independence, struggles against imperialism and its military blocs, against military bases on its territory; a state that struggles against new forms of colonialism and the penetration of imperialist capital. . . .[7]

In his book *Soviet Foreign Propaganda* Professor Frederick C. Barghoorn sees, as the title suggests, the Soviet emphasis upon imperialism as a propaganda message to ensnare the unwitting, particularly in underdeveloped nations. He quotes these instructions on the purpose of newspapers in 1961:

> In the exposition of international life and foreign policy the newspaper must constantly conduct propaganda for the foreign policy actions of the Soviet government, the struggle of the USSR for peace and the relaxation of international tensions, and must expose and uncover the imperialistic character of the foreign policy of the capitalist states and in particular of the United States of America. The most important obligation of the newspaper consists in convincingly conducting propaganda for the idea of peaceful coexistence of states with different social-economic systems, and of the struggle of the USSR for the prevention of a new war and the adjustment of disputed issues by negotiations, and the exposure of the plans of the capitalist states, directed against the USSR and the countries of peoples democracy and against the peoples fighting for liberation from colonialism.[8]

Undoubtedly there is a deliberate propaganda effort to sell the idea of capitalist imperialism, particularly to the people of Africa and Asia who lived for so long under foreign rule. Yet it would seem there is *some* element of genuineness to the claim. Communist ideology, indebted to Lenin, insists upon the imperialistic nature of capitalism. Even if this is granted to be a wholly untrue conception—and many there are who will state that there is at least an iota of truth to the idea that capitalism is imperialistic—that does not alter the fact that Communists *believe* it to be true.

Americans and Soviets, whether we like it or not, have at least one thing in common—supreme belief in their ideas. Americans see our land as the cradle of liberty, offering the best and truest way of life. The Soviets believe they have the true faith and it is their duty to bring it to the rest of the world.

We can now return to the question posed earlier: why did Americans hate and fear communism so? The answer is surely complex. We had never known the Russian people very well and understood them even less. We had a view, if only unconsciously, that they were a peculiar racial breed, backward, uncultured, uncivilized, and rather more animalistic. As Elihu Root observed, dirty they were.

The Communist revolution occurred during World War I. We were all wrapped up in "making the world safe for democracy." When the Bolsheviks took Russia out of the war, it seemed cowardly and definitely most undemocratic. It was dishonorable and dishonor was repugnant.

The Bolsheviks were a strange breed, constantly talking about the masses and claiming to represent them. (The very word "masses" affronted individualistic Americans.) They seemed to Americans to be brutal men, destroying what was beautiful and cultured in the

USSR, in order to commonize everything at the lowest possible level.

Some of the Bolshevik ideas were anathema to Americans. They were godless. Atheism was the official state religion. Organized religions and the devout in America were shocked by this at the time and have opposed it ever since. In the minds of America, the clash became one between the godly and the godless. We were on a holy crusade to defend God against those who would destroy Him.

The Communist ideas on the family disgusted Americans. There was much talk in America that the Reds had "nationalized" women; that is, that marriage had been abolished and all women were the property of all men, creating a circus of free love. We believed homes and families had been abolished, that Russians were herded into barracks where the sexes mingled and the nearest woman was the most convenient woman. This idea persisted in America long after Russian communism reverted to a type of sexual puritanism more straitlaced than any sexual conduct in America.

In short, communism was the enemy of civilization, the living denial of the grace of man, the abrogation of his higher instincts and motives. It was a return to the cave.

But these ideas, while commonly held, were peripheral to the real issues that caused fear in America. What bothered Americans most was the Marxist doc-

trine of class struggle, world revolution, and dictatorship of the proletariat. America honored property.
The idea that property would be taken away, handed
over to the state to be used by a bunch of radicals, was
a good bit more than Americans could stomach.

Marxist theory—The *Communist Manifesto* had
been written in 1848—had come to America long before the Bolshevik Revolution. It was well known to
radicals in the labor movement and consistently cited
by various Socialist labor leaders. Those who believed
in Marxist theories and urged them on the nation were
not called Communists or even Marxists in the late
nineteenth and early twentieth centuries. They were
known as anarchists or perhaps nihilists. These words
correctly mean people who believe in little or no government. But in America they came to be used much
as the word Communist was later.

One of the leading importers of Marxist theories was
Johann Most, a German radical, who emigrated to Chicago in 1882. In speeches and in articles in the radical
press, he urged workers to use violence against their
employers. He authored a pamphlet entitled *Science
of Revolutionary Warfare—A Manual of Instruction
in the Use and Production of Nitroglycerine, Dynamite, Gun-Cotton, Fulminating Mercury, Bombs,
Fuses, Poison,* etc., etc. Through the German language
newspaper *Die Arbeiter Zeitung,* Most and his followers urged violence:

Dynamite! Of all the good stuff, that is the stuff! Stuff several pounds of this sublime stuff into an inch pipe (gas or water pipe), plug up both ends, insert a cap with a fuse attached, place this in the immediate vicinity of a lot of rich loafers who live by the sweat of other people's brows, and light the fuse. A most cheerful and gratifying result will follow. . . .

In 1886, following a riot between police and strikers in Chicago, in which four men were killed and many wounded, *Die Arbeiter Zeitung* ran this headline:

BLOOD! Lead and Powder as a Cure for Dissatisfied Workers—This is Law and Order!

A handbill was circulated reading:

Revenge! Workingmen, to arms!!!

One of the results of this sort of inflammatory material was the famed Haymarket Riot in Chicago, in which police opened fire on peaceful demonstrators at a rally. There were heavy casualties on both sides.

America has a long history of labor violence, from the 1860s to the 1930s. There were pitched battles between strikers and company police, detectives, police, national guardsmen, and even federal troops. In his book *Radicalism in America,* Sidney Lens contends that labor violence was an American phenomenon:

Time and again workers in mass production industries and on the nation's railroads were driven to violence on a scale far outstripping anything in Europe.

No country in the world has witnessed so many picket line battles and so many deaths on picket lines as the United States. Figures are fragmentary to document this point, but a survey made by *Outlook* magazine in 1904 gives some idea of how extensive was this phenomenon. In the thirty-three months prior to the survey—not a particularly exceptional period—198 men were killed in picket lines in thirty states, 1,966 injured, 6,114 arrested.[9]

Perhaps only a couple of this large number of massacres of workers need be cited. Workers in Ludlow, Colorado struck the Colorado Fuel and Iron Company, owned by John D. Rockefeller. Evicted from their company-owned dwellings, the strikers moved into a tent city. To protect their families, a cave was dug inside the largest tent and thirteen children and a pregnant woman were harbored there. On Easter night, company police and national guardsmen poured oil on the tents and set fire to them. The woman and children perished in the conflagration, along with six others sprayed with gunfire.

This macabre event occurred in 1914, only three years before the Bolshevik Revolution. If America's fears of her own workers were so great as to lead to such massacres, can it be wondered that we feared the Bolsheviks who were urging the workers of the world to unite to destroy capitalism through revolution?

Long before the Bolsheviks were ever heard of, America feared anarchy and worker rebellion. During the bloody nationwide Pullman strike in 1894, newspapers fanned the tensions (some believed America was on the point of civil war) with headlines such as these:

ANARCHISTS AND SOCIALISTS SAID TO BE PLANNING THE DESTRUCTION AND LOOTING OF THE TREASURY.[10]

The violence of the Pullman strike was caused by the entry of federal troops into what had been a peaceful and effective strike against the Pullman Company, makers of railway sleeping cars. The United States Attorney General, Richard B. Olney, who ordered the troops in to break the strike, was a railroad lawyer and director of several rail companies.

The labor movement in America had plenty of Socialists, Marxists, and radicals, but the mainstream was represented by Samuel Gompers who headed the American Federation of Labor in the latter part of the last century. While sympathetic to many Socialist ideas, he was determined to keep the AFL centered on short-term goals of higher wages, better working conditions, and union recognition. Eugene V. Debs, the leading Socialist of the pre-World War I era, was a confirmed pacifist. He and Gompers joined to accept a harsh defeat in the Pullman strike rather than have the bloodshed continue or civil war come to America.

The point is not whether the anarchists and Marxists were powerful; the point is that American corporations thought they were or feared they might become so. Through manipulation of public opinion, the corporations convinced the majority of Americans of their viewpoint.

In 1917, when the Russian Revolution occurred, and on into the 1920s and 1930s, American industry was fighting organized labor. Virtually any means, fair or foul, was used by industry to keep the unions out. To have the Bolsheviks issuing calls for world revolution was hardly calculated to decrease the fears of American industrialists or to make them love the Communists.

There were legitimate reasons to dislike and distrust communism and its advocates, and these fears were fanned into hatred through scare campaigns.[11] By whom? There were many people: politicians such as Attorney General Palmer, church groups, newspaper editors, and other molders of public opinion. But surely *some* of the anti-Communist hate campaign originated with American industrialists who feared—legitimately from their point of view—that the Communists would inspire American workers to revolution. By attacking the Bolsheviks and communism, by labeling as Communist Socialists and other labor leaders of America, by encouraging violence against them and their arrests in Palmer-type pogroms, industrialists and capitalists hoped to prevent unionization of American industry, let alone any sort of revolution.

Communism was also considered a threat to the

American political system. In 1917 and for a long time afterward (even today!) the nation's economic and political systems were considered intertwined. Democracy and free enterprise went together in the American mind like stars and stripes. They were inseparable. We could not conceive of a Socialist democracy such as Sweden. What threatened free enterprise threatened democracy.

And the threat was real. The Communists avowedly and repeatedly made known their view that the American government was merely a tool of the capitalists. Their revolution was political as well as economic. Democracy (American style) had to be toppled in favor of democracy (Soviet style), and Americans correctly perceived that the Soviet system was rigidly totalitarian, the antithesis of the freedoms America believed in.

And so there came to exist two great nations, great in land, population, and economic potential, who were markedly different. One offered democracy and capitalism and a high degree of individual freedom; the other totalitarianism, state socialism, and little freedom. These differences were serious enough. Great efforts at trust and understanding would be needed to surmount them. But the problems were made impossibly greater by the foolish imperceptions each had of the other. Each was committed to an ideology. Each had the true gospel. Each had Right and Truth and Goodness.

Professor Stoessinger has written a superior exposition of the role imperception played in Soviet-American relations. He deserves to be quoted at length:

These self-images . . . determined the perceptions of the adversary's character. The Americans came to view the Bolsheviks with gradually deepening horror. At the time of the Red Scare, bolshevism had become the devil incarnate. Lenin and Trotsky, in turn, regarded the United States with increasing contempt, which, by the time of the intervention, had developed into a bitter and relentless hatred. Most Americans viewed the Bolsheviks as more wicked in their intentions than the old czarist regime. The czar, after all, had harbored no global ambitions. The Bolsheviks, however, preached world revolution and had established the Comintern in order to subvert the non-Communist part of the world. Similarly, Lenin believed that the United States, by virtue of its capitalist nature, would be driven inexorably to expansion and imperialism.

Finally, Wilson and most of his fellow-Americans viewed the Bolsheviks as a transitional phenomenon. There was the hope that they would be overthrown and that the intervention might speed the process. Lenin, too, saw the United States as a house divided and its power built on sand, ready to collapse under the determined onslaught of its workers.

This was the way in which two great peoples collided in the cauldron of world war and revolution. And this was how they started on a road that was to lead them to the brink of war. Neither Wilson nor Lenin was able to transcend his experience or to expand his vision. Each remained within his universe, and neither developed a sense of empathy for the other's destiny. Thus, neither could teach his people to reach out across the gulf that was to separate Americans and Russians for generations.[12]

4

THE TRAGIC YEARS: THE 1930s

THE POLICY OF non-recognition of the Soviet Union, begun by President Wilson, was continued under Presidents Harding, Coolidge, and Hoover. Not until 1933, shortly after Franklin D. Roosevelt entered the White House, did the United States begin to recognize the Soviets as the legal government of Russia.

This policy of non-recognition has been a rather consistent theme of American foreign policy toward Communist states. The Communists assumed power in China in 1949. The United States had not yet formally recognized that fact in 1972. During the years there were some meetings between representatives of the two nations in Korea and in Poland, but not until President Nixon's celebrated trip to Peking in 1972 were any sort of permanent contacts established. At this writing formal diplomatic recognition with exchanges of ambassadors has still not taken place. Similarly, the United States has refused to recognize the Castro government of Cuba, which came into power in 1959.

There may have been no formal diplomatic relations between the United States and the Soviet Union during the 1920s, but each certainly knew the other existed. There was, however, some informal recognition. In mid-1921, America reacted to the starvation and acute suffering of the Russian people by sending Herbert Hoover as head of a large relief mission. Several million dollars' worth of food and medical supplies were distributed among the people.

That may have seemed strange to many, for it came at a time when each side was carrying on a hate campaign against the other. What may have been the typical American viewpoint was expressed by Senator Henry L. Myers of Montana in a Senate speech in 1920:

> They have utterly destroyed marriage, the home, the fireside, the family, the cornerstones of all civilization, all society. They have undertaken to destroy what God created and ordained. They defy alike the will of God, the precepts of Christianity, the decrees of civilization, the customs of society. It is hard to realize that such things exist and are tolerated by the civilized world.[1]

If such was our attitude, why did we send relief? There were several reasons. Simple humanitarianism, surely. The Russian people were suffering after the revolution and from intervention by foreign powers. Particularly tragic were the *bezprizornye*—the hundreds of thousands, perhaps millions of children orphaned in the revolution and civil war. Most were homeless and lived by begging and stealing. Ultimately the Soviet government placed them in orphanages, boarding schools, and reformatories.

Another reason for the aid was our belief that the Russian people were oppressed by the Bolshevik tyrants. The aid would be a people-to-people effort, perhaps encouraging the Russians to overthrow their Red masters. At least it would let them know there were finer things in the world than communism. Hoover himself said in 1921 that "American charity had planted the American flag in the hearts of all those little ones and it is a greater protection to the United States than any battleship." [2]

Even more glowing (and unreal) was the statement by Colonel William N. Haskell in a report to Hoover:

> To the mind of the Russian common people, the American Relief Administration was a miracle of God which came to them in their darkest hour, under the Stars and Stripes. It turned the corner for civilization in Russia.[3]

Finally, the growing popularity of another American approach to the problem of communism provided a further reason for the aid: the capitalist dollar would do what denunciatory words and armed intervention had failed to do—topple the Bolsheviks. In 1921, Lenin had announced his New Economic Policy, a temporary retreat to state capitalism in which some private ownership and capitalistic incentives were permitted in industry and agriculture. Americans reacted with glee. The new policy was proof positive that communism would not work, that only American capitalism offered economic prosperity. The American relief aid was viewed as an effort to aid the cause of capitalism in Russia by showering the bounty of American capitalism on the wretched Russians.

Not surprisingly, the Soviet leaders greeted the American aid with distrust. Lenin never could understand why America would dispense charity while refusing to recognize his government. He accused the Hoover group of dispensing aid only to anti-Communist elements of the population.

Americans continued to crow about the triumph of capitalism through most of the 1920s. The United States was experiencing one of its peak economic periods, while the USSR was struggling simply to feed its people. Then the tables were turned with the Great Depression of the thirties. It was one of the worst and assuredly the longest depression in our history. Twenty-five percent of American workers were unemployed. There were bread and soup lines. Banks failed. The stock market hit bottom. It was now the turn of the American people to suffer.

The depression affected all of the Western world. All capitalist countries endured curtailed production and employment. World trade fell to a low ebb. The Soviet Union, in contrast, was relatively unaffected. They were only beginning to rise out of the chaos of the revolution and civil war and so had a lower economic base to start with. Their isolation from the rest of the world meant they were more self-contained. They had never been dependent upon world trade.

Consequently, the Soviets now had a chance to crow. And they did. In 1931, Politburo member Lazar Kaganovich brought a meeting of the Communist Youth League "to the verge of hysterical laughter" with this description of American economic problems:

> Even rich America, which thought it had found perpetual prosperity, is now so embarrassed by unemployment that a certain town recently decided to clear snow from its streets by men with shovels instead of with big machinery—to provide work for the unemployed. Whereupon one of the newspapers suggested that if providing work was what mattered, why not remove the snow with teaspoons and employ thousands more? [4]

The Soviets loved the American depression. It was absolute proof of the long-predicted death throes of capitalism. New and more urgent calls were issued for American workers to rise up and throw off their capitalistic masters. Capitalism was doomed, while communism was marching to victory. And not a few Americans agreed. The Communist party in America grew in strength. Communist influence in the labor movement increased. Many intellectuals became enamored with communism as an ideology. Some joined the Communist party or attended meetings of so-called Communist front organizations sympathetic to Communist ideas. At the very least communism was given serious study during the depression.

Yet in the deepest, most desperate days of the depression, Americans rejected communism. They relied once again on the democratic political processes to elect President Roosevelt in 1932. He began immediately to lead Congress to enact his celebrated New Deal reforms. The effect was to end, apparently forever, old-fashioned *laissez-faire* capitalism (in which governmental regulation or activity is minimal) and begin a form of state capitalism which exists today. Business, industry, and agriculture are largely privately owned in the United States, yet all are subject to a considerable degree of regulation through government spending, subsidies, taxation and, since 1971, wage and price controls.

Communism also changed in the Soviet Union, in some ways more massively than had capitalism in America. Lenin died in 1924. The American reaction was perhaps best expressed by the *United Presbyterian*. "The great beast has gone down into the pit! Glory be to God!" [5]

We believed communism died with Lenin. Hardly. After a power struggle with Trotsky, who was exiled and later murdered in Mexico, Joseph Stalin emerged as the Soviet dictator. Stalin was a far different man from Lenin. In many ways he made Lenin look like a saint.

Stalin was not a Russian. The Russians are the largest of the scores of ethnic groups which make up the Soviet Union. Stalin was a Georgian from the south of the country. Unlike Lenin and Trotsky he was not a scion of a bourgeois family. Stalin's father had been a cobbler and Stalin belonged to the proletariat. Lenin had found it difficult to see how communism could succeed without world revolution. Stalin, while all in favor of the revolution and eager to promote it, was determined that communism should succeed in a single nation, even if the USSR was a most unlikely place. He was thus more nationalistic than Lenin. He was also shrewd, brutal, ruthless, suspicious, and distrustful.

There is no need here to review the history of Stalin's dictatorship. Only the major accomplishments that affected Soviet-American relations need be mentioned. Stalin cemented his personal control over the Soviet Union and all facets of the government, and he ruled with an iron hand. He controlled the Communist party, the only one permitted in Russia. Through the party, the Russian people, in large or small groups, were indoctrinated into Communist ideology. Propaganda campaigns, for whatever purpose, became a fixture.

He vastly enlarged the secret police, which infiltrated all aspects of Soviet life, including the army. Dissent was permitted until a decision was made by Stalin; then it was a Siberian prison or death for dissenters or the weak of will. He permitted no one to rise to enough power to even remotely challenge his authority. There were periodic purges in the bureaucracy, army, press, universities, and other aspects of Soviet life. The purges led to what Americans considered phony trials at which officials confessed their wrongdoings and were quietly led away. These were perhaps the fortunate ones, for it became a fixture of Soviet life for people simply to disappear, never to be heard from again. Fear became a fact of life. Later, after Stalin's death, he would be denounced for his terrors and for fostering the "cult of the personality."

Stalin reversed Lenin's New Economic Policy's dalliance with capitalism in favor of stringent state socialism. Agriculture had long been (and in the opinion of many still is) the greatest economic problem of the Soviet Union. Although the population was overwhelmingly peasant, not enough food was produced to feed the non-farming population. Lenin's policy had sought to correct this by providing capitalist-style incentives to small farmers (called Kulaks) to be productive on their own land.

Stalin reversed this and began a ruthless program of

forced collectivization. The Kulaks were removed from their land and forced on to immense collective farms, owned and managed by the state. There was great opposition, for land is to a farmer as the sea is to a fisherman. But Stalin crushed the opposition. It is believed today that millions of Kulaks were killed or died in prisons during the collectivization process.

The Russians who survived the purges, secret police, and collectivization were for a long time little better off. Stalin embarked on an ambitious program to lift the Soviet Union into the twentieth century economically. The bulk of Soviet production went into heavy industry—steel, basic metals, mining, machine tools, transportation, electric power, fuels—and most of what was left over went into the military forces. The people were deprived of food, housing, clothing, and all but the essentials of life. (Extensive education, health, and other social programs were offered, however.) Consumer production was almost nil. Wages were low and there was little to spend them on. Meanwhile, women as well as men worked at hard physical labor, and all were constantly exhorted to work harder and produce more.

It worked. Slowly at first and then with ever increasing acceleration, the Soviet Union grew economically. Today, despite its setback in World War II, the USSR economy is ranked second in the world and in some areas rivals the United States. Such progress had to occur, for, as we have seen, Stalin did by totalitarian methods what capitalism had done a century and a half before through the profit motive. They had both deprived the workers in order to invest profits in the means of production.

Stalin did not differ from his predecessors in at least one respect. He wanted diplomatic recognition from the United States. Pride of recognition was certainly a reason, but a minor one. Diplomatic recognition would permit an embassy to be established in Washington. This would permit greater opportunity for contact with the Communist party in America and make subversion easier. But trade was the major reason. Russia desperately needed American machinery and motors in exchange for ore and raw materials. The rise of militarism in Japan and nazism in Germany created a still more cogent reason.

There was growing agitation in the United States for recognition of the Soviet Union. In the opinion of Professor Stoessinger, "reality" was overcoming the imperception with which Americans had so long viewed the Soviets. We still hated and feared the Communists as godless and the enemy of property and democracy, but some hard facts of life were being considered.

The Soviet government showed no signs of going away. The thousands of Americans who traveled to the USSR came back with the opinion that the Communists, as dreadful as they might be, were firmly entrenched in power and that the people, as deprived as they might be, considered themselves better off than they had been under the tsars. It thus seemed rather ridiculous to many informed Americans to continue the policy of non-recognition. They believed we might as well face up to the existence of Russian communism and find a way to get along with it.

Too, the threat of Communist subversion in America began to seem greatly exaggerated. Even in the depression, Americans had clearly rejected communism and revolution. The Soviet system just didn't have much appeal to Americans, even when they were in their worst economic straits.

And, most important, America also needed trade with the Soviets. Our stagnant production needed the boost of world trade. If we could sell goods to the Russians and thus increase production and employment, it wasn't really important how godless and undemocratic they were. In short, we didn't have to like them to trade with them. It was a pragmatic American business attitude.

Agitation for recognition of the Soviet Union began in the late 1920s. Republican Senator William E. Borah of Idaho was among the prominent men urging recognition. It finally came in 1933.

Historian William Appleman Williams, in his book *American Russian Relations, 1781–1947,* speaks of the years between 1933 and 1939 as the "tragic" years in Soviet-American relations. He presents, as others have, a detailed study of how the United States, Britain, and France denied all appeals by the Soviet Union for collective action against the aggressions of Japan, Germany, and Italy during the 1930s.

Another author, Professor Frederick L. Schuman, was most outspoken in his book *Soviet Politics At Home and Abroad*:

The aggressions which led to the agonies of the early 1940s [World War II] were made possible by the military resurgence of Japan and the Nazi Reich during the 1930s. Fascist aggrandizement and mobilization for global conquest were made possible by the attitudes and actions of the social elites and political leaders of Great Britain, France, and the United States. The drift toward doom could have been halted only by suppressing any aggression anywhere through prompt collective action by all the non-Fascist powers. This had been Woodrow Wilson's formula for keeping the peace. It was also the formula of Litvinov, Molotov* and Stalin. It was repudiated in Washington, Paris, and London where Fascist aggression was met not with resistance, but with acquiescence or connivance.

Far from deserting the enterprise of collective security, the Communists in the Kremlin, alone among contemporary rulers, served the cause until the last possible moment and hoped against hope to the end that a common front could be achieved. The cause was lost. In the sequel, all that is meaningful and hopeful in Western culture entered into the valley of the shadow and was saved from death only by the suf-

---

* Maxim M. Litvinov, Soviet foreign commissar and ambassador to the United States in the 1930s, and Vyacheslav Molotov, foreign commissar who succeeded him.

fering and sacrifice of millions. This disaster was the fruit of the failure of America, Britain, France, and the USSR to act together in time. To assess blame for the catastrophe is not an academic exercise in historical analysis or moral judgment. It is the only possible way of avoiding new catastrophes in the future. The verdict of the record is unmistakable and obvious: responsibility for the breakdown of collective security rests on the Western democracies, not on the Soviet Union.

The melancholy details of the record need no restatement, save as they bear upon the situation in which the USSR found itself by 1939. Eight times during the preceding eight years the aggressors posed to the Western democracies a test of their willingness to organize and enforce peace. Eight times the Soviet Union called for collective action against aggression. Eight times the Western Powers evaded their responsibilities and blessed the aggressors.[6]

The eight times listed by Schuman: (1) Japanese seizure of Manchuria in September 1931; (2) Hitler's repudiation, in March 1935, of the disarmament clauses in the Treaty of Versailles ending World War I; (3) Italian invasion of Ethiopia in October 1935; (4) Hitler's seizure and remilitarization of the Rhineland between France and Germany in March 1936; (5) the Fascist attack, in which Germany and Italy participated, on the Spanish Republic in July 1936; (6) the Japanese attack on China in July 1937; (7) the Nazi seizure of Austria in March 1938; and (8) the Nazi seizure of Czechoslovakia in 1938.

The tragedy of these years is too long a story and has been told too often for detailing here. But we can glean from it some elements which greatly affect Soviet-American relations to this day.

The Soviet Union early perceived the threat Japan and Nazi Germany posed for it. The vast land of the USSR stretches from the Pacific facing Japan to the Polish plain facing Germany. Tsarist Russia had lost a war with Japan in 1905. The expansionist intentions of Japan in the Far East were unmistakable to Soviet leaders. The ambitions of Nazi Germany were even more apparent. In his book, *Mein Kampf,* Hitler had stated that the destiny of Germany and the Aryan race lay to the east—Poland and the Soviet Union. His hatred for the Russians was expressed. In his rise to power he had fanned hatred for Communists along with the Jews. All democracy was subjugated and dissent silenced in Nazi Germany in the middle thirties in the name of anti-communism.

There can be no doubt that the Soviets did sincerely try to alert Britain, France, and America to the dangers of Germany, Italy, and Japan and to institute collective action to stop their aggressions before the three nations grew militarily strong. Certain it is that the Russian actions were not motivated by love for liberty or objection to totalitarian forms of government. The Soviets were motivated simply by self-preservation. They knew they were to be eventual victims of aggression and wanted American, British, and French help to prevent it.

The United States, Britain, and France are not very proud of their failure to take collective action in the 1930s. Though it is no excuse, it is a fact that all three countries failed to realize the ambitions of Germany and Japan and the threat they posed to the free world. The Allies wanted peace and believed that peace could be achieved through negotiation and through appeasement of the aggressive appetites of the Fascist dictators.

There is another reason which we are less willing to admit, but which the Soviets considered paramount then, and today. We wanted the Fascists to destroy communism. Western leaders had read *Mein Kampf*, too. If a militaristic Germany turned eastward against the Soviet Union, it might not be a bad thing. According to Professor Schuman, Winston Churchill, who became Britain's valiant wartime prime minister, said in Rome, in 1927:

> Italy has shown that there is a way of fighting the subversive forces which can rally the masses of the people, properly led, to value and wish to defend the honor and stability of civilized society. She has provided the necessary antidote to the Russian poison. Hereafter no great nation will go unprovided with an ultimate means of protection against the cancerous growth of Bolshevism.

In 1934, Lloyd George, who had been Britain's leader in World War I, told the House of Commons:

In a very short time, perhaps in a year or two, the conservative elements in this country will be looking to Germany as the bulwark against communism in Europe. . . . Do not let us be in a hurry to condemn Germany. We shall be welcoming Germany as our friend.[7]

Many similar quotations could be given, but the point is undeniable that there were major elements in Britain, France, and the United States who believed that nazism and communism would turn on each other in war. It would be the best of all possible worlds if they destroyed each other in the process.

It was a gross miscalculation. Hitler turned on France and Britain in the West, largely destroying them, before attacking the Soviet Union in the East. In the long run, the tragedy of the thirties led to the distrust and cold war of the postwar era. The souring of Soviet-American relations in the thirties has continued to the present.

5

WORLD WAR II ALLIES

THE UNITED STATES and the Soviet Union were military allies during World War II. Both fought Germany with every ounce of their strength, and for the Russians it came very close to being their last ounce. They cooperated in fighting the war and sacrificed a great deal for each other.

Yet the events leading to their becoming allies were strange, some of their conduct as allies was odd, and the aftermath to the war has been surely tragic. All this might be briefly characterized by saying that the mutual distrust, based upon imperception, which began in 1917 and was nurtured in the 1920s and 1930s, never fully disappeared, even at the height of their wartime collaboration. At war's end, it returned with a vengeance.

Read in hindsight, the events leading up to World War II have all the makings of a Greek tragedy. World War II was an incomprehensible tragedy. Its cost for man, his civilization, and his humanity will never fully be calculated. Knowing what that war was, it is almost a form of suffering to read the detailed diplomatic history of the last few weeks prior to the start of the war in September 1939. The nations sped dizzily along an insane, unreal path toward nearly total destruction of what they were, knew, and loved.

The full story is now well known and many times told. It need not be done again here. Suffice it to say that after the Munich conference in 1938 in which Britain and France, with American acquiescence in the background, surrendered Czechoslovakia to Hitler, the world knew Poland was next. In July and August, European diplomats, knowing war was inevitable and certain it would come over Poland, frittered away their last chance to do very much about it.

Britain and France backed the Poles. It was obvious to all that Poland could not defend itself or be defended without the help of the Soviet Union. Yet the Poles, torn between their equal hatred for the Germans and the Russians, refused to allow Soviet troops to be based in their territory or to travel through it. The British were the major culprits. They knew that only a coalition of strength could thwart Nazi ambitions in Poland, yet they refused to remonstrate with the Poles. As Professor Schuman, writing in 1946, the year after the war ended and long before important documents were made public, put it:

> Chamberlain's [Neville Chamberlain, the British prime minister who had appeased Hitler at Munich] "coalition" thus consisted of a passive France, an impotent Poland, a helpless Greece and Rumania, and a Turkey unwilling to act. Without Soviet participation, said Lloyd George, these commitments were "sheer madness." [1]

At the root of Chamberlain's "mad" policies was his vain hope that somehow Germany would fight the Soviet Union and that they would destroy each other, while Britain, France, and Western Europe sat on the sidelines clapping with glee.

The greatest absurdity in the tragi-comedy of errors came on July 31, about a month before the war began. An Anglo-French mission was sent to Moscow to work out an agreement for mutual defense of Poland. The British sent a "wholly undistinguished" admiral, as Schuman charitably described him, Sir Reginald Plunkett-Ernle-Erle-Drax. He and General Joseph Doumenc of France traveled to the Soviet Union by slow boat, arriving on August 11. Even then they had no authority to sign any agreement.

A week later the Soviet Union and Nazi Germany signed a trade agreement. In another five days, on August 23, 1939, the two totalitarian nations signed a treaty of non-aggression.

To Americans the agreement was proof of Russian perfidy. The totalitarian Soviets were not one wit different or better than the totalitarian Nazis. It was only natural that Hitler and Stalin, two dictators as despotic as the world has ever known, should join hands against freedom and democracy.

The Soviets, who were eventually attacked by the Nazis in June 1941, long insisted they had no other choice. Their efforts at collective action through diplomacy had failed. The British and French refused to deal seriously with them as the eleventh hour approached. Their only recourse was to look out for themselves. This meant, as a beginning, the pact with Hitler to gain time to prepare for defense against Germany. Even then there was not enough time. Averell Harriman quotes Stalin as saying in his presence, "If Hitler had only given me one more year." [2]

A sensible account of the reasons for the pact was given by Schuman as early as 1946:

> Every Great Power . . . can seek safety amid the perils of the world anarchy through (1) security by supremacy, involving the liquidation of all possible rivals; (2) security by coalition, involving alliances with the least menacing among other Powers against the most menacing; or (3) security by balance, involving neutrality while others fight, plus an intention to intervene on behalf of the weak against the strong in the event that the strong threaten to effect a dangerous upset in the balance. Moscow had abandoned No. 1—i.e., World Revolution—because it

was unobtainable and because continued efforts to attain it fostered a coalition of all other Powers against the USSR. Moscow had embraced No. 2, but found it unworkable because of the attachment of the Anglo-French appeasers to No. 3 in a form favorable to the Axis [Germany-Italy-Japan] and perilous in the extreme to the Soviet Union. Moscow finally embraced No. 3 in a form favorable to the Axis and perilous in the extreme to France and Britain.[3]

The non-aggression pact with Hitler was the least the Soviets did. After Germany invaded Poland, scoring a quick victory, the Russians invaded from the east, taking fully half the country, eighty thousand square miles compared to seventy thousand for Germany, 13 million people compared to 22 million in the Nazi-occupied lands. Germany and the USSR soon reached agreements on a common "friendly" border. Stalin, much to Hitler's indignation, declared the Baltic nations of Latvia, Lithuania, and Estonia to be part of the Soviet sphere of influence. Hitler accepted the affront from Stalin only because he considered Soviet domination of these lands an entirely temporary condition.

The Soviets took one other major step to prepare for the war they knew was coming. The border of Finland was only twenty miles from Leningrad. The Russians wanted Finnish territory to enlarge their defense area. Attempts were made to obtain the land through negotiation. The Soviets offered to exchange territories, but the deal was unsatisfactory to the Finns. They were asked to surrender their Mannheim Line, which defended them against the USSR, and control of the Gulf of Finland and Lake Ladoga, for territory they were not much interested in.

The Finns refused and war resulted. From late November 1939 to mid-January 1940, the Finns fought the Red Army to a standstill, inflicting heavy casualties. Americans were thrilled that the valiant "democratic" (there was a significant pro-Nazi element in Finland) Finns were defeating the Red "hordes." The United States became convinced of the utter ineptitude of the Red Army. More accurate information was that Moscow had not expected war with Finland and was ill-prepared for it. When preparations were made, Finland was quickly crushed.

The non-aggression pact with Hitler, the march into Poland, and the war against Finland, all taking place in 1939–40, convinced Americans of what they already knew, that the Soviets were a perfidious, dastardly lot bent on bullying and conquering smaller, helpless nations on their borders.

With hindsight, another conclusion may be reached. Through these efforts, the Soviets gained almost two years in which to prepare for war, without which the results of the war might have been entirely different. Hitler's armies came within a whisker of defeating the Soviet Union, as it was. Without those two years, the Germans would surely have crushed the Red Army, gained control of the vast resources of the USSR, and been well on their way to their goal of world conquest.

There are those who have another view: that Stalin did not really believe Hitler would attack him and was unprepared for war. One piece of evidence for this conclusion is that Stalin did not mobilize the Red Army prior to the German attack, despite the fact that both the British and the Americans had informed him they had intelligence information that the attack was imminent. Apparently Stalin believed the information was a trick to get him to mobilize, thus providing Hitler with an excuse to attack the Soviet Union. There are also reports that Stalin was so surprised by the attack that he became completely unnerved and took several days to grasp control of the situation.

Hitler attacked Russia on June 22, 1941, nearly six months before the United States entered the war following the Japanese attack on Pearl Harbor, Hawaii. The Nazi forces attacked in overwhelming strength, had great success, gobbled up immense amounts of Russian territory, and caused inconceivable destruction. Yet it is safe to say that the Germans lost the war in the Soviet Union. Britain and the United States might have had an impossibly difficult time defeating Germany if the USSR had collapsed. Doubtless, only the A-bomb dropped on Germany would have turned the tide.

War, like many endeavors, includes miscalculation, error, and chance, as well as brilliance and courage. Generals, admirals, and military historians who have great interest in these matters believe Hitler lost the war in the East at the outset because he began his Russian offensive six weeks late. The Italians were supposed to conquer Greece. But the Italian army was so inept and the Greek forces, aided by the British, so stubborn that German units had to be dispatched to subdue Greece. The delay cost six weeks. It is widely believed that if the Germans had had those six weeks in the fall before the heavy snows came, they would have taken Moscow and all of the Ukraine, putting the war beyond the Soviet Union's reach.

Others believe that even with the delay Hitler would have won if he had concentrated his forces to take Moscow. The theory is that Moscow is the nerve center of the Soviet nation. With it gone, the Soviets supposedly would have had a much more difficult time continuing the war. As it was, German forces never did take Moscow, nor did they capture Leningrad, although they laid siege to it for nine hundred days.

Still others think that neither the Germans nor anyone else could have won a land war in the Soviet Union. The country, one-sixth the land mass of the earth, is so vast there is no way to conquer it or to control it if its 200 million people are in opposition. The Germans came from the West. Where would they stop to claim a victory? Moscow? The Ural Mountains? Or would they have to go all the way to Vladivostok on the Pacific?

The Russians seemed to fight with this strategy in

mind, using the land and the bitter Russian winters to punish and then defeat the Nazis. Some Red Army units were overrun and smashed in the initial German blitzkrieg offensive which reached to the gates of Moscow and deep into the Ukraine, the "breadbasket" of Russia. But in the main the Red Army retreated, leaving "scorched earth" which could offer little sustenance or shelter to the Germans.

Hitler believed the Wehrmacht was winning. There were hundreds of thousands of Russian prisoners, many of whom died as a result of the torture and suffering in Nazi prison camps. Hitler's army scored victory after victory, destroying equipment and cutting into the Soviet Union as though it were butter. But when the snows stopped the advance the first year, the Germans, ill-prepared for winter weather, were stunned when the Red Army seemed to rise out of the snow, equipped with large numbers of tanks and guns.

There was another German offensive in the summer of 1942, but the Russians stood and fought finally at Stalingrad * on the Volga River in September 1942. It was the mightiest battle of the war, with millions of men deployed on each side. Hitler ordered his forces to take the city at all costs, and Stalin commanded his men to defend it at all costs. Each house and building became a battleground. After two months, the Germans had taken most of the city, but the Soviet garri-

* Renamed Volgograd in 1961, following the death and downgrading of Stalin.

son, supplied from the east bank of the Volga, held out. That courageous stand gave the Red Army time to mount a counteroffensive, which attacked the Germans from the north and south, seeking to encircle and trap the Nazi army. Hitler refused to allow his generals to withdraw and the circle was closed. An estimated three hundred thousand Germans were lost in the battle. Russian casualties were greater.

For the Germans the war was lost right there, although it lingered on amid rivers of blood for almost three years. After Stalingrad, the Red Army generally maintained the offensive. It grew in strength and at war's end was draining three German divisions for every one committed to the Western Front.

The German invasion of the Soviet Union made the latter an instant ally of Britain, which was fighting virtually alone against Germany. Six months later, when the United States entered the war, Communist Russia and capitalist America became allies.

Following the attack on the USSR, Churchill told the British people in a radio broadcast, "Any man or state who fights on against Nazidom will have our aid . . ." Privately he expressed a more genuine attitude to an associate, "If Hitler invaded Hell, I would make at least a favorable reference to the Devil in the House of Commons." [4]

Britain desperately needed the Soviet Union. All of continental Western Europe, save neutral Sweden, Switzerland, Spain, and Portugal, had been lost. Britain had saved the remnants of its expeditionary force in France through the miraculous evacuation at Dunkirk. It fought on, desperate for weapons, behind the shield of its navy, protected by its diminutive Royal Air Force. The British were brought to their knees by the German air assaults, but rallied by Churchill, they fought on.

There is much speculation that Hitler believed the British would approve of his attack on the Soviet Union, but he miscalculated the growing British hatred of nazism. The British and then the Americans considered Hitlerism a far greater evil than communism. The evilness of communism was lost, if not entirely forgotten, in the all-consuming enmity toward nazism. Few since have disagreed with that attitude.

It is hard to remember today (and inconceivable to many) how much we Americans loved the Soviets during the war. We admired their courage in defeat and cheered their victories, although the war on the Eastern Front seemed awfully far away. Hollywood ground out propaganda films saluting Russian courage in the midst of suffering. Americans were fascinated with things Russian and a Red Army marching song made the Hit Parade. Stalin was affectionately known as Uncle Joe.

But even so there were a few prickles in Soviet-American relations. A major one was lend lease, as American aid to both Britain and the USSR was called, even though few ever expected to be repaid. The name had been attached to American aid before this country entered the war. It stuck even though armaments, food, and other materials shipped abroad were a part of our war effort. As the war ground on and the Red Army stood at Stalingrad and then fought back to victory after victory, Americans came to believe that only American aid saved the Russians from defeat. This was a way of saying that America indirectly won the war on the Eastern Front. We simply could not conceive of communism ever producing enough guns, tanks, and planes to defeat the Nazis.

The issue has never been settled. The Soviet Union desperately needed American aid. They could not have won without it. And massive amounts of it were shipped there. Between October 1, 1941 and April 30, 1944, the United States shipped 8,872 aircraft, 3,734 tanks, 206,771 trucks, 3,168 anti-aircraft guns, 5,500,-000 pairs of army boots, and 2,199,000 tons of food. The total amount of materiel received from the United States totaled 7.4 million tons.[5]

The cost in casualties of getting these tremendous shipments to the Soviet ports of Murmansk and Archangel was great. The American-British convoys had to travel through a rain of German torpedoes and bombs. Losses were horrendous. One convoy had twenty-three out of thirty-four ships sunk. A southern route through the Mediterranean was developed and aircraft were flown from Alaska to Siberia, but even so America paid a high price in lives just getting the materiel to the USSR.

The American materiel was important to the Russian victory, yet there can be little doubt that Americans exaggerated its importance. Soviet industry, Communist though it was, produced the majority of the war materials for the Red Army. Our insistence that it was otherwise was symptomatic of our continuing imperception of the Soviet Union.

American aid was a bone of contention between the Soviet Union and the United States. Averell Harriman described a meeting he and Britain's Lord Beaverbrook had with Stalin in September 1941. This was after the German invasion of Russia, but before Pearl Harbor. Wrote Harriman:

> We had three long talks [with Stalin] on successive evenings. During the first meeting he discussed the military situation and his urgent requirements, and Beaverbrook and I outlined what was available from British and American sources. Stalin appeared so agreeable that Beaverbrook was elated and thought our job was almost done. In the second talk, however, after Stalin had a chance to review what we had said with his colleagues, he was brutally critical, claiming gruffly that *the paucity of our offers was proof that we wanted the Soviet Union defeated.* (Emphasis added)
>
> It was hard sledding. He argued about individual items, about which he was particularly concerned. He refused to accept our explanations. For example, at one time he turned on me saying, "Why is it that the United States can only offer one thousand tons of armor plate for tanks, a country with a production of over fifty million tons of steel?" He brushed aside my explanation of the length of time required to increase

capacity for this type of steel, saying, "One only has to add some alloys."

Beaverbrook and I left the meeting puzzled and somewhat discouraged. We decided to give Stalin during the third talk, as a response to the list of Soviet requirements they had given us, an itemized statement of categories of equipment and material we believed we could furnish. Stalin evidently felt he had put as much pressure on us as he could and now accepted our offer with good grace. He even showed enthusiasm. He emphasized the urgent need for trucks, particularly three-ton trucks were "the most desirable." "Our bridges can't carry any heavier," he said. He also expressed concern about barbed wire. I assured him we would give his requests full consideration and do all we could.[6]

The major issue of disagreement among the three wartime Allies was the opening of the second front. Stalin began demanding it in late 1941 from the British and after American entry into the war from both countries. The reason for it was obvious. The Soviet Union was carrying the burden of the ground war. It was fighting the bulk of the German Wehrmacht single-handedly and suffering most of the casualties. A second front would pull German troops away from the east, make it easier for the Russians, and end the war sooner.

But the task was not easy for the Anglo-American Allies. To invade the German fortress from the west or south meant an amphibious landing, a most difficult military undertaking. A vast sea armada would have to

be prepared to land enough troops and supplies to prevent the entire force from being driven into the sea by
a much smaller number of German defenders.

In July 1942, Churchill journeyed to Moscow to talk
with Stalin about the second front. Averell Harriman
was present and has described his impressions:

> Churchill had to undertake to explain that the sec-
> ond front in Europe, the cross Channel operation, was
> not possible in 1942. He described why the required
> build-up of forces in the United Kingdom and from
> the United States with the necessary landing craft
> could not be accomplished until the following year.
> Stalin argued with him at every turn, disputing
> Churchill's figures on German forces in the west and
> claiming that their divisions were under-strength—
> "only two regiments apiece." He said that his views
> about war were different: "Any man who is not pre-
> pared to take risks cannot win a war."
> Churchill agreed but asserted it would be folly to
> waste troops which would be needed for a successful
> operation next year.[7]

The British prime minister then told of British-
American plans to invade North Africa in October.
Stalin eventually became enthusiastic about the plan,
but not until he and Churchill "argued," as Churchill
himself put it, for an extended period. At one point
Stalin taunted Churchill by saying that the British
should not be afraid to fight the Germans.

Britain and the United States did invade North Africa in 1942 and Sicily and Italy in 1943, but Stalin was dissatisfied with these efforts until the second front was established in France in June 1944. Nazi Germany surrendered less than a year later in April 1945.

The suspicion lingered throughout the war that Stalin believed the British and Americans were not giving their all, as were the Russians. Americans suspected that he did not fully appreciate the American effort involved in fighting both Japan and Germany, halfway around the world from each other, or the British and especially American effort that went into the bombing of Germany during 1943 and 1944. The United States always maintained it had aided the Russians immeasurably with the bombing of German industry. The Soviets believed they bore the brunt of the war.

These disagreements over military aid and second fronts were only symptomatic of what really made America's alliance with the Soviets strange during the war. The two nations were united in the sense that they sought to defeat a common enemy. There was considerable military cooperation. American pilots were permitted to land on Soviet airfields. When British and American troops landed in Normandy, the Russians launched a major offensive in the East, as requested, to keep the Germans occupied there.

Yet there was never any unified military command with the Soviets such as the British and Americans had under General Eisenhower or as the British, French, and Americans had had under Marshal Foch in World

War I. The Russians fought their war in the East and the British and Americans fought theirs in the West. At best they compared notes on what was happening and congratulated or commiserated with one another. Besides, the Soviets did not aid the United States in its difficult war with Japan by declaring war and engaging in any military action in the Far East until the very final stages of the war against Japan, when the help was hardly needed. The Russians were not asked to fight Japan and, indeed, could not have for a long time, so hard-pressed were they by the Germans. Still, all these things made it an alliance of convenience, not of the heart.

6

REMAKING THE WORLD AT YALTA

STALIN, CHURCHILL, AND ROOSEVELT began planning the peace well before the unconditional surrender of Nazi Germany and Japan. The Big Three met at Teheran, Iran, in November 1943 and at Yalta in southern Russia in February 1945. Roosevelt and Churchill had several separate meetings at which the postwar peace was discussed.

Viewed from the hindsight of a quarter century, one can only marvel that these three old men, all born well before the turn of the twentieth century, believed that they could take into their hands the scraps of the world left at the conclusion of the war and mold it into a good thing that would provide peace for generations. It is amazing that they tried at all, which they did mightily, and a true marvel that they succeeded as well as they did. Despite a nearly constant succession of small conflicts and interminable tensions and threats, the big bang has not occurred.

Consider the state of the world in 1945. The vast majority of Americans, living an insular existence, were scarcely aware of it. Most of the economically productive parts of the world were in ruins—all of Western Europe including Britain, eastern Russia, North Africa, and the bulk of Asia, including Japan, China, and the Philippines. South America, black Africa, and the subcontinent of India were largely untouched, but they were either inept or just arising from colonialism.

The United States stood alone as a super colossus—economically, militarily, politically. Britain was an allied victor, but she was exhausted, never to rise to great power status again. France was in a similar condition, only worse, for there was the shame of defeat, capitulation, and collaboration with the Germans. Proud Frenchmen have difficulty living with it to this day.

The Soviet Union? Stalin went to great pains to conceal the fact, but the nation was in desperate straits at war's end. Her population had declined by twenty-four million from 1941 to 1945. An estimated twenty million Russian lives, or 10 percent of the population, were lost in the war. This percentage would have been the equivalent of the United States losing sixteen million lives during the war. Vast portions of its most productive terrain were in ruins. The industrialization and modernization accomplished at so fearful a price prior to the war were largely undone. Steel production, for example, was cut in half. Soviet agriculture was wholly incapable of feeding the nation.

In contrast, the United States was largely unscathed by the war. It had been unbombed, uninvaded. Its people were healthy and secure and, despite wartime rationing, Americans lived in luxury compared to Europeans. American military might was unrivaled. Its army, navy, and air force had fought two wars halfway around the world from each other, vanquishing stubborn, fanatical enemies. There was an American general in Berlin as well as Tokyo. And, above all, we alone had "the bomb." Economically, we were ahead of all the rest of the world. Our factories had supplied the British and Russian armies, as well as our own. We were a powerhouse of production. We seemed also to have all the money in the world. In short, the world was in a lopsided condition, with one superpower and the rest of the world in poverty. Many historians believe that if Americans ever realized that fact they did not appreciate it and above all did not make use of it.

When Stalin, Churchill, and Roosevelt met at Yalta, they undertook the superhuman task of remaking the world. A generation of postwar Americans was told of the "perfidy" of Stalin at Yalta and of Roosevelt's "weakness." Yet it is not too soon to state that all three were sincere and tried mightily to do the impossible.

Consider briefly some, though not all, of the problems. The three men were radically different in background, attitudes, and desires. They were prisoners of their pasts and the histories of their respective nations. Even Roosevelt and Churchill, fast friends though they were, disagreed over Churchill's dedication to the British Empire. They disagreed over the purely military conduct of the war, making the Anglo-American military effort at best a series of compromises to avoid dissension. Add dictator Stalin, the Communist economic and political ideology, and the language barrier and the possibilities for threefold agreement were reduced to nil.

The threesome had a war to conclude. They had to find a way to solve the disastrous economic problems that were the war's legacy. They had to remake the map of the world, find some way to demilitarize Germany and Japan, give substance to the desires of small nations, care for the disadvantaged people who were only beginning to reach out for nationalism, preserve important national interests of each nation, placate divisive political groups within their own countries, and much more. Above all, they had to do all this and preserve some semblance of unity among the three wartime allies.

The verdict of history, I believe, will be amazement at how much they accomplished, not how little.

They met at Yalta, three men well aware that they were shaping the world for generations to come. The idealism and naïveté of it all is touching when considered today. They met for long hours during the day and at night gathered in convivial banquets in which scores of toasts (mostly in watered vodka) were drunk to mutual friendship and the glowing future. Near the end of the conference, Churchill made this toast to Stalin:

> I have drunk this toast on several occasions. This time I drink it with a warmer feeling than at previous meetings, not because he is more triumphant, but because the great victories and the glory of the Russian arms have made him kindlier than he was in the hard times through which we have passed. I feel that whatever differences there may be on certain questions, he has a good friend in Britain. I hope to see the future of Russia bright, prosperous, and happy. I will do anything to help, and I am sure so will the President. There was a time when the Marshal [Stalin] was not so kindly towards us, and I remember that I said a few rude things about him, but our common dangers and common loyalties have wiped all that out. The fire of war has burnt up the misunderstandings of the past. We feel we have a friend whom we can trust, and I hope he will continue to feel the same about us. I pray he may live to see his beloved Russia not only glorious in war, but also happy in peace.[1]

Then, it is embarrassing to read today, Edward Stettinius, the American secretary of state, spoke. John Toland records it this way:

Stettinius turned to Stalin in an excess of sentiment and enthusiasm. "If we work together in the post-war years, there's no reason why every home in the Soviet Union couldn't soon have electricity and plumbing."

"We have learned much already from the United States," Stalin replied without the trace of a smile.[2]

There was a great deal that was unreal and pathetic at Yalta. Here were three old men, one of whom (Roosevelt) would soon die and another (Churchill) be toppled from power by elections in his nation, acting on the basis of gross imperceptions of themselves, their power, and the world they sought to change.

Winston Churchill, one of the builders and certainly a cardinal champion of the British Empire, could not realize that the empire was dead. He could not see that the two world wars had exhausted the British nation or that within a few years the great empire would dissolve under a wave of nationalism. At Yalta, Britain was already a second-rate power with neither the power nor the energy to maintain its empire or play a co-equal role in world affairs with either the Soviet Union or the United States. Yet Churchill joined Roosevelt and Stalin in wry, quite catty remarks about the arrogance and pretensions of General Charles DeGaulle of France. Churchill could see the second-rate status of France, but not of his own nation.

Franklin Roosevelt, the supreme American politician, the master charmer, believed he could win Stalin's cooperation in the postwar world with little more than the force of his own remarkable personality. Not surprisingly, Roosevelt and Stalin did get along. Stalin seemed to like the President personally. He apparently had genuine admiration for him, believing the social changes Roosevelt had wrought in the United States under the New Deal ranked with the accomplishments of Lenin in the Soviet Union. There is evidence that he was amazed that Roosevelt had done it by peaceful means.

Roosevelt was successful in charming Stalin. Cordiality there often was. High-minded words flowed from both their lips. But in the end, Roosevelt allowed the words to substitute for deeds.

Roosevelt carried an incredible naïveté with him to Yalta. Toland's book, *The Last 100 Days,* contains this passage:

> The former ambassador to Russia, William C. Bullitt . . . feared that Roosevelt was being taken in. Roosevelt, he remembered, had once told him in private that he would convert Stalin from Soviet imperialism to democratic collaboration by giving him everything he needed to fight the Nazis. Stalin needed peace so badly, the President had said, that he would willingly pay for it by collaborating with the West. Bullitt predicted that Stalin would never keep his agreements.

"Bill, I don't dispute your facts," Roosevelt replied. "They are accurate. I don't dispute the logic of your reasoning. I just have a hunch that Stalin is not that kind of a man. Harry [Hopkins, a key Roosevelt advisor] says he's not and that he doesn't want anything but security for his country, and I think that if I give him everything I possibly can and ask nothing from him in return, *noblesse oblige*—he won't try to annex anything and will work with me for a world of democracy and peace." [3]

The illogic and naïveté of that statement is astounding. If it was true that all Stalin wanted was security for his country—and many believe it was true—then how could it be expected that Stalin would seek it other than through annexation of nations bordering the Soviet Union? And how could giving Stalin what he wanted and asking nothing in return possibly convert a totalitarian dictatorship into a democracy? And doesn't Roosevelt's whole attitude smack of pre-war appeasement of Nazi Germany?

Roosevelt was a prisoner of the past at Yalta. How? The ghost of Woodrow Wilson stalked the conference hall. Wilson, the idealist, had conceived the League of Nations after World War I, but the United States had not joined. And Americans, Roosevelt foremost among them, felt guilt. If we had joined the League and taken an active part in the consultations of nations, we might have prevented the catastrophe of World War II.

Roosevelt's chief interest at Yalta was the founding of what eventually became the United Nations. He considered it a triumph that Stalin agreed to join such an organization on terms that were reasonably acceptable to the American people. At first, Stalin had wanted sixteen votes, one for each of the republics in the Soviet Union. This would have been equivalent to the United States demanding forty-eight votes, one for each state that existed at the time. When Stalin agreed to settle for three votes, Roosevelt considered the negotiations eminently successful.

Roosevelt, indeed all of America, failed to see that no international organization could keep the peace if the great powers did not keep peace among themselves. But we were in love with peace and international cooperation. We believed our own words about the brotherhood of man. We loved our own rhetoric about the goodwill of men. Naïve we surely were. Pragmatic we were not.

Joseph Stalin strode through the conference like a dinosaur among elves. He demanded, he objected. He explained his nation's fears. He sought security. But in realistic terms. His nation had twice been invaded by Germany in his lifetime. He wanted, not assurances, but protection, buffer states, friendly neighbors,[4] money in the form of reparations from Germany to rebuild his country, and much more. He was prepared to get these by every means he could. In the diplomatic bargaining at Yalta he was determined to gain for what he gave. He would happily join a United Nations, but he wanted a friendly, Communist government in Poland, some Polish territory, a neutralized Germany, German reparations in return.

Nothing that occurred at Yalta is more illuminating than Stalin's haggling with Roosevelt over a warm-water port in the Far East in return for Russian entry into the war against Japan. Roosevelt gave him the Kurile Islands north of Japan and a variety of warm-water ports were discussed.

And Stalin, too, was a prisoner of the past. A warm-water port had been a goal of the tsars from ancient times. Dominance over Eastern Europe was an old Russian wish dressed up in Communist attire.

Stalin went to Yalta to bargain, to horse trade—and not from strength but from weakness. Roosevelt and Churchill, veteran politicians surely, either failed to understand this or to take advantage of it. Both seemed afraid of Stalin and the Soviet Union. They worried about his cooperation both during and after the war. They ended up sometimes offering him more than he'd ever hoped to gain by bargaining. Professor Adam B. Ulam, in his book *The Rivals,* described this, referring to the 1943 Big Three conference at Teheran:

> In their separate ways Roosevelt and Churchill went far in appeasing their awesome partner. In the

vain hope of obtaining Russian concurrence to a
modification or postponement of the massive invasion
of Northern France, Churchill initiated a discussion
of the Polish problem in terms which probably surpassed Soviet expectations. Roosevelt ostentatiously
took Stalin's side in some disputes with Churchill and
tried to jolly him up. Thus, between his two partners
and their different anxieties and approaches, Stalin
was able to dominate the conference. In reading its
proceedings one is struck by how much of it consisted
of *his* demands and *his* requests for explanation,
while the leader of the most powerful country in the
world and the prime minister of the country which
had held out alone for more than a year were usually
on the defensive. (His emphasis)[5]

7

FROM
ALLIES TO
ANTAGONISTS

AMERICA IS A polyglot nation with a host of racial, religious, and ethnic groups and a government of special interests—corporate, labor, business, veteran, educational, racial, agricultural, and a great many more.[1]

To rise to power in America, be it in large municipalities, states, or the federal government, a politician must learn to form a majority out of this diversity. He must learn the arts of compromise. He must discover how to offer the diverse elements at least half a loaf (or a few large crumbs) in exchange for their support. He must master the pragmatic political arts of give and take, face saving, and seeming to say "yes" while meaning "no." As the old political saying goes, he must know how to straddle a fence while keeping an ear to the ground—and that isn't very easy.

Whether we like it or not, the aim of the American political process is the finding of such men. American presidents are master politicians. Yet these same men have a tendency to act as babes in the woods when they enter international politics.

Consider Franklin D. Roosevelt. History may prove that he was the master politician of all time in America. Physically a cripple, he was elected to the nation's highest office four times. He affected a generation of American politics. He forged a majority of racial, ethnic, labor, and intellectual groups which has not entirely disappeared more than a third of a century later. He made the Democratic party numerically dominant in the land. He had all of the political arts in abundance. He is in many ways the yardstick by which all his successors have been measured. Yet in foreign affairs he was naïve.

There were differences in style, but Roosevelt attacked postwar problems much as Wilson had done, with idealism. Wilson had his Fourteen Points, Roosevelt his Four Freedoms. Both were making the world safe for democracy. Both men, in wartime, were capable of inspiring Americans to the most untoward sacrifice for victory, but neither knew how to make a peace. More correctly said, neither knew how to fight a war to make a peace.

On the other hand, Stalin, who had less need to be a domestic politician, fought the war politically as well as militarily and succeeded perhaps far beyond his dreams. And Churchill often, though not consistently, saw the political implications of the war and tried to compete, but his nation lacked the strength to act on his own good sense. Roosevelt, leading the most powerful nation, had only a scanty conception of international politics.

The evidence for this evaluation is plentiful. Stalin and Churchill, both products of nineteenth-century European politics, saw the world in terms of spheres of influence. From Stalin's point of view, Britain had its empire and its Commonwealth nations of Canada, Australia, New Zealand, South Africa, and others. The United States had a sphere of influences in North and South America and, doubtless as a result of the war, throughout the Pacific and Japan. Stalin wanted his. He thought it natural, indeed Churchill had suggested it. Chances are he found it difficult to understand why the Americans should object to it.

Stalin's sphere of influence, as he saw it, was twofold. First was Eastern Europe—the former Baltic states, Poland, and the Balkan states of Rumania, Bulgaria, Yugoslavia, Albania, Hungary, perhaps Austria and Czechoslovakia. In the Far East, the Soviet sphere should include Mongolia, Manchuria, and China, along with Afghanistan, Iran, and Turkey in the Near East. All these lands were not only logical spheres of influence, they also offered the protection of space. Russia had twice in a generation been invaded through Poland and the Balkans. From a Soviet point of view, it made sense for these lands to be "friendly neigh-bors," which meant Communist-dominated.

Stalin set out to accomplish this in war. His armies would give the Soviet Union an area of dominance. Seweryn Bialer points this out in *Stalin and His Generals*.

> Victorious Soviet armies were hammering out a Soviet sphere of influence. The strategy of the Soviet Armies, now that the enemy was almost completely pushed out of the territory of the USSR, was clearly influenced by political considerations. Memoirs of Russian military commanders offer testimony. On October 28 [1944], Marshal Malinovski was called to the telephone and informed by Stalin that Budapest had to be taken forthwith. The commander of the Soviet armies in Hungary explained that other operations appeared for the moment advisable and less likely to incur prohibitive casualties. No, insisted Stalin, *political considerations* made capture of Budapest imperative, no matter what the cost in lives.[2] (Emphasis added)

In contrast American forces gave little or no consideration to politics. Churchill, far more conscious of postwar political considerations than Roosevelt, begged for the troops of the Western Allies to advance as far to the east as possible. He wanted the American and British troops to take Berlin, as much of Germany as they could, Prague in Czechoslovakia, and Vienna in Austria—more if possible. Eisenhower, the Allied commander, refused on military grounds. The casualties would be high and needless, and the cost of feeding the liberated peoples would be enormous. Eisenhower was backed in this decision by General George C. Marshall, the chief of staff of the United States Army. Roosevelt, his friendship with Churchill notwithstanding, backed his military commanders. Upon Roosevelt's death in April 1945, President Truman took the same line.[3]

American troops actually stopped for several weeks —field commanders such as General George Patton chafing all the while—to await the arrival of Soviet troops. General Eisenhower later admitted it was a huge mistake. The political map of Europe would have been greatly changed, the postwar problems vastly different had American troops plunged ahead to garner as much territory as possible.

But Americans did not think in those terms. We were simply winning a war, scoring a military victory over an unmitigated evil which was nazism. The purely political considerations of what was to happen after the war never entered our thoughts. Indeed, in our idealism, we did not *want* them to enter.

Yet when Stalin's USSR carved out a sphere of influence in Eastern Europe, creating half a dozen Communist-dominated states, we reacted with dismay. We believed in democracy, which we were making the world safe for. We believed in self-determination of peoples. We believed in free elections in which people would elect their leaders. To us this was what the war and its sacrifice were all about. When the Soviet Union grabbed this terrain and imposed dictatorships and communism upon it, we were disillusioned. Our sphere of influence in the Western Hemisphere and the Pacific, we believed, was a product of democracy and self-determination. The Soviet sphere in Eastern Europe was a product of land-grabbing imperialism. We saw the world as bad and good, Communist and democratic.

Consider Poland. It was a pawn in the international chess game that began well before the war ended. The American people had long had a special affection for Poland and the Poles. It was the land of Chopin and Paderewski and we believed the Poles had a special thirst for freedom. The creation of a self-governing Polish nation following World War I had pleased Americans greatly. Free at last after centuries of tyranny, Poland was also a matter of political importance in America. The United States had a significant Polish population. Their votes counted and no American office-seeker could ignore the "Polish question," let alone oppose a free, independent Poland. It is perhaps not an exaggeration to state, moreover, that the Poles were a symbol to Americans of man's aspirations for freedom. We had similar feelings for the Latvians, Lithuanians, Estonians, Hungarians, Rumanians, Croats, Serbs, Bulgars, Slovaks, and Czechs, but perhaps few would disagree that the Poles stood first in the hearts of Americans. We wanted a free Poland.

The British had similar ideas. In Churchill's words,

Britain had "drawn the sword" over Poland, whereas it had permitted the Austrians and Czechs to come under the Nazi yoke undefended. Britain, too, wanted a free Poland.

Stalin had different ideas. The Poles and the Russians had never gotten along. The Polish boundaries, created artificially following World War I, included significant numbers of people who belonged ethnically to either Germany or the Soviet Union. To Stalin, Poland had far less viability as a nation than it did to the Americans and British.

More importantly, Russians saw the Polish plain as a road through which Germany had twice invaded their country. Bent on security, the Soviets were not about to leave it paved again. They preferred to annex the large piece of Polish territory they had invaded in 1939. Failing in that, or perhaps in addition to it, they wanted a "friendly neighbor" in Poland—which meant a Communist, Soviet-dominated government.

During the war, while Germany occupied Poland, two provisional or Polish governments in exile existed. There was the Free Polish government in London, made up of officials from the pre-war government who had escaped the Nazis. Britain and the United States recognized this government. The Russians, somewhat later in the war, created the so-called Lublin government, which was Communist.

The Polish question revolved around which of these two governments was to control Poland after it was liberated and what the boundaries of the reconstituted Polish nation were to be. The question of postwar Poland was raised frequently during the war. Roosevelt was particularly concerned about the matter, as Harriman points out:

> On Roosevelt's instructions I discussed the future of Poland with Stalin more often than any other single subject. Once, in March, 1944, when I raised the subject Stalin said impatiently, "Again the Poles? Is that the most important question?" He added that he had been so occupied with the Poles that he had had "no time for military matters." I replied that the Polish question "was pressing." I pointed out that the American public opinion would not support a "handpicked" government for Poland and that the Polish people should be "given a chance freely to choose their own government." Stalin replied that he was "concerned about public opinion in the Soviet Union." As our talks had been exceedingly direct I commented, "You know how to handle your public opinion." He answered, "There have been three revolutions[4] in a generation." Molotov, who rarely interjected himself into the conversation, added, "In Russia, there is an active public opinion which overthrows governments."[5]

Stalin's statement to Harriman is illuminating for it became known after the war just how "occupied" the Soviets were in Poland. The Russians joined the Nazis in a systematic deflowering of the Polish nation. Millions of Poles, including most of its large Jewish population, were slaughtered by the Nazis. The USSR joined in eliminating anti-Communist elements. At Katyn Forest, the Soviets are believed to have massacred an estimated forty thousand Polish army officers.

Then there was the Russian role, or more accurately non-role, in the famous Warsaw uprising which began August 1, 1944. In a tragic effort to liberate Poland from the Nazi yoke and to establish a free government before the Russian army arrived in Warsaw, the Polish government in London ordered the 35,000-man Polish underground army to revolt and drive out the Nazis. The Germans reacted with a savage attack on the Poles with the aim of destroying the underground and Warsaw with it.

The poorly armed Poles fought house-to-house with great courage. The uprising lasted for eight weeks before it was crushed with the loss of more than 200,000 Poles. The Warsaw uprising remains to this day a symbol both of human courage in the quest for freedom and the inhumanity of oppressors. The world was moved in 1971 when Willy Brandt, the leader of democratic West Germany, knelt at a monument to the Warsaw dead and openly wept in grief over the atrocities the German nation had perpetrated a quarter century before.

Where was the Soviet Union during the Warsaw uprising? The Red Army was across the Vistula River within easy striking distance of the beleaguered Poles. And it did nothing. It did not attack in an effort to reach Warsaw or at least divert German troops from their grisly tasks. Indeed, Soviet gunners did not even fire on German planes which were dive-bombing the Warsaw ghetto—and the planes were well within range. Perhaps worse, Stalin refused to allow American planes, which hoped to drop supplies to the Polish garrison, to land on Soviet airfields.

Churchill and Roosevelt begged Stalin to attack to aid the Poles, but he refused, making the dubious claim that his forces were under attack, too, and the Red Army could not free Warsaw. Few historians believe Stalin. Rather, his actions indicated that he wanted the uprising to fail, the underground to be crushed, and the democratic elements in Warsaw demoralized prior to Russian occupation. In reply to the entreaties of Roosevelt and Churchill, Stalin wired:

SOONER OR LATER THE TRUTH ABOUT THE HANDFUL OF POWER-SEEKING CRIMINALS WHO LAUNCHED THE WARSAW ADVENTURE WILL OUT. THOSE ELEMENTS, PLAYING ON THE CREDULITY OF THE INHABITANTS OF WARSAW, EXPOSED PRACTICALLY UNARMED PEOPLE TO GERMAN GUNS, ARMOUR AND AIRCRAFT. . . .[6]

After the Red Army "liberated" Poland, the Communist Lublin government was placed in power. There was little Roosevelt and Churchill could do but entreat Stalin to permit free elections to give the Poles self-determination. Stalin held the elections, although they hardly coincided with Western ideas of a free election, and the Lublin government won.

Much the same pattern was followed in the Balkan nations, while Latvia, Lithuania, and Estonia became "republics" of the USSR. By war's end, Stalin had his sphere of influence in Eastern Europe.

That was not all. Although independent, Finland was strongly dominated by the Soviet Union. Threats were being made against Iran and Turkey. Greece faced a powerful Communist insurgency. There were strong Communist parties throughout Western Europe.

In the Far East, the Soviet Union seemed to be a great bear gobbling up vast terrain. The USSR had not entered the war against Japan until a week before it ended, and to a generation of Americans it seemed unnecessary for the Russians to enter at all. America had fought the war against Japan largely alone. With much of its fleet destroyed in the Japanese attack on Pearl Harbor, the United States Navy had fought some of the great naval battles of history against superior Japanese forces and won them. With great courage, American soldiers had fought for lonely Pacific islands, eventually regaining the Philippines and bases for the air offensive against Japan itself.

The American military thought that the Japanese would not surrender without an invasion of the Japanese home islands. The Japanese had proven themselves to be fanatical. Their most effective weapon had become the kamikazes—bomb-laden planes crashed into American ships by Japanese suicide pilots. American military officers believed the invasion of Japan would be monstrously difficult, that the Japanese would defend their homeland inch-by-inch and that American casualties would be enormous. The war could conceivably go on for years.

Americans wanted Soviet entry into the war against Japan. A major concession by Stalin at Yalta had been his promise to enter the war as soon as Germany was defeated. Even at the Potsdam Conference held between July 17 and August 2, 1945, after the end of the war in Europe, President Truman[7] asked for Russian entry into the Japanese war. Truman persisted in this request even though he received word while at the conference that the atomic bomb had been successfully tested at Los Alamos, New Mexico.

To a generation of Americans, Russian entry into the Far Eastern war—with its tragedies lasting to this day—was a sellout. But in defense of both Roosevelt and Truman, it must be said that neither had any way of knowing the effects of the bomb. To Roosevelt, the Manhattan Project (the code name for construction of the bomb) was at best a hope and at worst a risky scientific scheme. No one could be certain that the bomb could be built or that it would work, let alone how effective it would be. Truman learned at Potsdam that the test had been a success, but even then he could not be certain of the bomb's effects on Japan. The invasion of Japan was still believed necessary. Participation by the Red Army would, therefore, save American lives.

Hindsight leads to the sellout theory. The bomb was dropped at Hiroshima and Nagasaki and the Japanese quickly surrendered. A subject of controversy ever since 1945 is whether the bomb was needed at all. Japan was being brought to its knees by conventional bombing raids. Tokyo had been virtually destroyed without the atomic bomb. Important elements in Japan were urging surrender before the bomb was dropped. Still, there were fanatical groups in Japan who wanted to fight to the death, bomb or no bomb.[8] In the end, the issue was decided by Emperor Hirohito, who ordered surrender to save his people greater suffering.

Professor Ulam argues, in a highly appealing fashion, that America's great mistake in the Pacific was its demand for unconditional surrender by the Japanese. We equated Japan with Nazi Germany, when the facts were otherwise. Japanese militarism was more of an accident of history. Japan did not have the strategic position Germany had in Europe. Certainly, there was in Japan no form of racist ideology similar to nazism. Ulam maintains that Japan had long since been beaten by American military might, despite the fact that much of the effort had gone into the war in Europe—so powerful was the United States. If we had accepted surrender on some terms less than unconditional, Russian entry into the war could have been avoided. As it was, we did accept conditions—the preservation of the life of Hirohito.

The week-long Russian entry into the war has plagued America ever since. The Russians occupied Manchuria in the north of China, and systematically raped it of its industry. North Korea became a Communist nation, following Russian occupation. The Communists under Mao Tse-tung in China were immeasurably strengthened in their civil war to overthrow Chiang Kai-shek. The war in Vietnam is a direct legacy of the Russian entry into the war against Japan.

There was more. The Russians got the Kurile Islands north of Japan. They asked for a zone of occupation, Hokkaido Island, in Japan. Truman agreed, but insisted that American General Douglas MacArthur remain supreme commander. Since this was an intolerable situation for the Russians, they never took the zone. At one point, the Russians were even bargaining for an air base in the American-owned Aleutian Islands, so they could set up an air route to Seattle—something incomprehensible at the time.

Russian entry into the war against Japan may be considered an American tragedy. We have fought a three-year war in Korea and a seemingly endless war in Vietnam. China has become Communist and militantly anti-American. The people of the United States may well cry, "If only the Soviets had been kept out of the war in the Far East." But that "if only" does not take into consideration what seemed to be the realities of 1945. Yet the sellout theory of Yalta and Potsdam became anti-Communist gospel in America.

Americans reacted with dismay that quickly turned to revulsion at the Soviet imperialism in Europe and the Far East. The Soviet Union seemed out to grab all it could from the ruins of war. And everywhere it assumed control it imposed a totalitarian Communist society. Individual liberty was eliminated and all opposition leaders were "liquidated" (a popular word in America synonymous with "killed"). All became secret societies with secret police in control. Democracy died.

To Americans it seemed that all we had fought for had come to naught. The peoples of Eastern Europe and the Far East had simply traded Nazi chains for Communist fetters. Our hopes for an orderly, peaceful, democratic world were smashed. We came to hate the Russians and communism as much as we had nazism.

The actions that followed, known as the cold war, will be described shortly. At this point we need to try to understand what was happening and speculate on what else America might have done in the circumstances.

The Soviet Union and the United States viewed each other and the world with imperception and the results were tragic. At the very least, each failed to understand the other or even to try to understand.

At war's end, the Soviet Union looked out upon a hostile world in which it was rather weak. The USSR had been ravaged by the war. It had a large and powerful ground army, but that in itself was a weakness, for its manpower was desperately needed in civilian life to help rebuild the nation.

The Russians viewed a world in which the United States was overwhelmingly powerful. We, too, had a large and powerful ground army. Our navy and air force exceeded those of the rest of the world combined. Moreover, we had the ultimate weapon, the bomb, and we had it exclusively. Our armies were spread over most of Western Europe. The Pacific Ocean had been virtually reduced to an American lake. Moreover, America was an economic colossus.

This view of the world situation, and accurate it was, led to the Soviet actions for perhaps two major reasons. First, to the Russians it must have seemed they were taking very little—a few not very valuable lands in Eastern Europe and the Far East. On a map they might seem huge, but none was considered economically advanced. All were war-torn. In a sense they offered more of an economic liability than an asset, at least for the immediate future.

In comparison the United States had its traditional dominance in the Western Hemisphere, to which it had added dominance over Western Europe and virtually the entire Pacific. China was still under Chiang Kai-shek, and he was considered highly loyal to America. To the Soviets, it must have seemed that their sphere of influence was small and insignificant compared to America's. Surely, they wondered what we were objecting to.

Second, the Soviet view was colored by Leninist thought. Capitalist nations were natural, inevitable enemies of Communist nations, which—in the Russian view—offered the true, ultimate utopia for man on this earth. Moreover, capitalist nations, being in their death throes, turned imperialistic. World War II could be seen as the imperialism of capitalist Germany gone berserk, only to meet defeat in the snows of Communist Russia. To Stalin and the Communist theorists it was only natural that capitalistic America, now so powerful, should turn imperialistic.

American avowals that they wanted no territory as a result of the war—even if believed—were unimportant, for American imperialism could be economic. The American dollar, supreme in the world, could dominate as surely as the sword, subjugating industries, nations, and peoples. Indeed, the American dollar did dominate the world following the war.

The Russians wanted reparations from Germany, which is to say they wanted the Germans to pay for the damage done to the Soviet Union during the war. There was considerable discussion of this at both Yalta and Potsdam. The Americans and British came finally to realize that it was self-defeating to saddle a devastated Germany and Japan with huge reparations debts. That had been done after World War I with repercussions that led to world depression and World War II. This was not the Russian view, however. They must have found it difficult to understand why we objected to their dismantling and taking to the Soviet Union the available factories of East Germany and Manchuria. It was a pittance compared to what the United States possessed.

Worse, our opposition to the truly paltry Soviet sphere of influence and to its picayune seizure of reparations must have seemed to them evidence of our unyielding hostility. America had opposed the Communist revolution. We had invaded Russia hoping to overthrow the Bolsheviks. We had conducted hate campaigns. Our lack of cooperation in the Soviet Union's schemes for the postwar world and our open opposition to what the USSR did seemed to them evidence of American imperialism. Everything we did from their point of view proved our desire to see communism destroyed. We had not conspired with Nazi Germany, as Stalin had long feared, for the defeat of the USSR, but we were bent on the same ends by different means after the war.

To most Americans such Soviet attitudes, if understood at all, were pure rubbish. We possessed in democracy and capitalism the true faith that would lead to a better world. We had absolutely no territorial ambitions and disliked anyone, including the British, French, and Dutch, who entertained them. Our occupation of Germany and Japan, our trusteeships of the Pacific Island, were a form of national sacrifice for a better world, a sort of white man's burden. If we gave economic aid to other nations, it was for their benefit, again a form of sacrifice. If we benefited economically from our sacrifice, it was again in the best interests of other nations.

The Russian sphere of influence, its buffer states against a German invasion, was imperialism pure and simple. We sought no sphere of influence. We were just helping others. The Soviets were simply subjugating other nations which had a right to self-determination and democracy and freedom and free enterprise. If those nations chose in free, American-style elections to be Communist—unthinkable surely—that was one thing, but to deny such processes by force of arms was proof of Russian imperialism.

Our view of Communist ideology enforced this belief. Didn't the Communists believe in world revolution? Weren't they constantly trying to stir it up around the world, even in the United States? The Russian land grabs following the war proved that communism was an imperialistic evil, devoted to subjugating men and nations. America must stop it. We had failed to act against Nazi Germany and Japan. World War II had been the result. We should not make the same mistake again and permit Soviet imperialism to accomplish what Hitler had failed to do. Not a few came to believe that America had fought on the wrong side during the war. Others held that both nazism and communism were unmitigated evils. We should use the bomb and destroy the USSR while we were still on top.

Thus, the two most powerful nations on earth quickly came to confront each other in hostility. Each saw the other as an inherent evil, an object of distrust, bent on world domination. And each nation used hatred against the other for national purposes. For the Soviets, anti-Americanism was used to goad the war-weary Russians into accepting continued privation and back-breaking work to rebuild the nation and compete with the United States economically. In America, anti-communism was used to ensure that Americans did not backslide into pre-war isolationism, but rather took an active role in international affairs.

The question is whether either campaign was necessary. The Soviet Union would have been rebuilt out of sheer necessity. The Stalin regime, as it had demonstrated prior to the war, had ample means to spur its people into sacrifice and work. Anti-Americanism was hardly needed. There was also goodly evidence that Americans had forsaken isolationism. We had participated in the war and postwar decisions. We had joined the United Nations, lavishing on it our hopes for the future. Americans were convinced that our pre-war policies of isolationism and appeasement had been a tragedy. No less an isolationist than Senator Arthur Vandenberg of Michigan, chairman of the Senate Foreign Relations Committee following the war, had announced his sincere conversion to internationalism. Our position in the world as the only source of the economic aid desperately needed in Europe assured our continued involvement. Finally, American troops occupied Germany and Japan. Anti-communism was hardly necessary to ensure our involvment.

Yet the hate campaigns were mounted in each nation as instruments of national policy. A fragile peace was fractured into hostility, tension, the cold war, Korea, Vietnam, and much more.

Could it have been any other way?

This is surely an exercise in speculation, for it didn't happen, but there is usefulness in pursuing answers, if only as a means of perhaps learning from past mistakes. One line of speculation is that the United States should have been more pragmatic and tough-minded at Teheran, Yalta, and afterward. We held most of the playing cards in the deck, and we should have used them to further the goals we sought. If Roosevelt and Truman had been less idealistic and naïve and simply played international politics as competently as they did domestic politics, they might well have been able to parlay American military and economic power into such goals as a free Poland and self-determination for peoples. Roosevelt's efforts to "jolly up" Stalin were surely useless.

Such speculation is perhaps wishful thinking. The Red Army swept into Poland and the Balkans. The

United States had no way to dislodge them short of open warfare. But if Roosevelt had engaged in more hard bargaining, as Stalin did, the United States might have obtained more in return for the Soviet sphere of influence than a promise to join the United Nations and to enter the Pacific war. At the very least, Stalin might have gotten an impression of American intransigence which could have caused him to hesitate in his land grabs.

Another area of speculation has the United States issuing an ultimatum to Stalin to back away from Poland and the other nations he ensnared. According to this theory, the Soviet Union was so weak and fearful of war that Stalin would have had to permit the United States at least to share in the occupation of the Eastern European lands.

But that, too, is wishful thinking. Roosevelt certainly had no way to predict that Stalin would become so uncooperative. And, enlarging the Allied zones of occupation would surely have brought Russian troops into Western Europe and prolonged American troop commitments to Europe for longer than anyone thought conceivable in 1945.

Still a third view is that Americans should have tried harder to understand the Russians and their fears of Germany and the United States. We should have granted them their spheres of influence, aided them economically in their recovery, tried to demonstrate to Stalin that his intransigence toward America was unnecessary, and sought to cooperate with the Soviet Union in every way possible. The United States and the USSR could have tried to be more like friendly rivals than frightened antagonists.[9]

This, too, is wishful thinking, for ideology and public opinion in both nations, bathed in imperception and tempered by the past, simply could not tolerate such ideas. Cooperation was just too difficult.

Perhaps it is just as well that none of these possibilities became reality. There are a large number of professors and foreign affairs analysts who, while opposed to American policies today, heartily applaud those of the immediate postwar era.

8

THE
TRUMAN
DOCTRINE

It is the consensus of modern historians that Harry S. Truman, who succeeded to the White House upon the death of Franklin Roosevelt in April 1945, ranks with Washington, Lincoln, Wilson, and Roosevelt as a "great" president. In a television interview in August 1972, as conservative a Republican as Senator Barry Goldwater of Arizona (who ran for president in 1964) called Democrat Truman "the greatest president of this century."

Such accolades are not based upon Truman's personality or appearance. He has always been a plain and simple man, unpretentious, direct of speech, and wholly courageous. As president, he was not much of an orator and entirely lacked charisma. Television became a popular medium during his administrations, yet he was never very good on it, and his election in 1948 certainly owed nothing to it. Perhaps his major appeal as a political campaigner was his fighting spirit. He reminded people of a fighting cock with never-say-die qualities. In 1948, his audiences used to holler, "Give 'em hell, Harry," and he did. The slogan is a fixture in American politics today, with only the name changed.

Truman brought to the White House a considerable knowledge of history and great respect for the office of president. He believed it was his duty to make decisions. He made some monumental ones, then stuck by them, and worked for them with great energy and courage.

His most important decisions were to drop the A-bomb on Japan and to set up the Atomic Energy Commission; the building of the hydrogen bomb; a strong military posture for America; formation of the Central Intelligence Agency and our worldwide spying apparatus; the Korean War; the firing of General Douglas MacArthur who commanded it; formation of the Truman Doctrine; the Marshall Plan for the economic recovery of Europe; and creation of the North Atlantic Treaty Organization (NATO). All these were in the field of foreign affairs. They form a rocklike foundation for greatness.

Harry Truman formulated American foreign policies which have been followed with only minor revisions by each of his successors—Eisenhower, Kennedy, Johnson, and Nixon. These are high credentials for greatness, but it is no disrespect for Mr. Truman to suggest that the test of greatness demands longer than a quarter century. He would probably have been among those who would agree with that.

The Truman policies, as carried out by himself and his successors, have led to war, great loss of life, much bloodshed, inconceivable expense, continuous cold war[1] tensions with the Soviet Union and other Communist nations, division among the American people, and vast changes in the American form of government. It will remain for the historians of fifty or one hundred years from now, when the cold war will probably be a near historical curiosity, to decide if the Truman policies were wise and necessary or foolish and tragic—or some of each.

The Truman Doctrine has been America's major postwar policy. It has led directly or indirectly to the wars in Korea and Vietnam, and to our interventions in Laos, Cambodia, Thailand, Guatemala, Dominican Republic, Cuba, and Lebanon. Our military preparedness and our thousands of military bases around the world are part of its legacy.

But it is important to remember that the Truman Doctrine, announced by Truman in an appearance before Congress on March 12, 1947, began in a small and limited fashion. It was the American answer to what we considered Soviet threats against Greece and Turkey. Stalin was demanding large portions of Turkish territory, as well as the right to help the Turks police the Dardanelles and Bosporus straits, which offer the Russians access from the Black Sea to the Mediterranean Sea. In Greece, a weak and ineffectual pro-Western regime, bolstered by British aid and fifty thousand troops, was losing ground against armed Communist insurgents operating from bases in Albania and Yugoslavia.

The problem reached the crisis stage for American leaders when the British informed them that they were no longer able to carry the burden of economic and military aid to prop up the Greek regime. The United States would have to take over.

Truman acted with characteristic decisiveness. He returned on March 7 from a meeting with the president of Mexico and a speech in Texas to meet with Dean Acheson, who was then his under secretary of state. In his memoirs, *Present at the Creation*, Acheson described how quickly the Truman Doctrine was formed.

Deciding that he had no alternative but to go ahead, and realizing that this was only a beginning, he approved a request for two hundred and fifty million dollars for Greece and one hundred fifty million dollars for Turkey, and the message to Congress. We then moved into the Cabinet Room, where the President laid out the whole program, which got unanimous Cabinet support, and ordered a meeting with congressional leaders for March 10, and, depending on its outcome, a presidential appearance before Congress on March 12. I came back to the Department [of State] somewhat breathless. When President Truman had made a decision, he moved fast.[2]

The rationale for the Truman Doctrine was given personally by Acheson to the congressional leaders. He has described his role with considerable flair and drama:

My distinguished chief,[3] most unusually and unhappily, flubbed his opening statement. In desperation I whispered to him a request to speak. This was my crisis. For a week I had nurtured [4] it. These congressmen had no conception of what challenged them; it was my task to bring it home. Both my superiors, equally perturbed, gave me the floor. Never have I spoken under such a pressing sense that the issue was up to me alone. No time was left for measured appraisal. In the past eighteen months, I said, Soviet pressure on the Straits, on Iran, and on northern Greece had brought the Balkans to the point where a highly possible Soviet breakthrough might open three continents to Soviet penetration. Like apples in a barrel infected by one rotten one, the corruption of Greece would infect Iran and all to the east. It would also carry infection to Africa through Asia Minor and Egypt, and to Europe through Italy and France, already threatened by the strongest domestic Communist parties in Western Europe. The Soviet Union was playing one of the greatest gambles in history at minimal cost. It did not need to win all the possibilities. Even one or two offered immense gains. We and we alone were in a position to break up the play. These were the stakes that British withdrawal from the eastern Mediterranean offered to an eager and ruthless opponent.

A long silence followed. Then Arthur Vandenberg said solemnly, "Mr. President, if you will say that to the Congress and the country, I will support you and I believe that most of its members will do the same." [5]

There is another view of the Greek situation set forth by Richard J. Barnet in his book *Intervention and Revolution.* He maintained that Washington

　. . . developed a rationale to justify a moral crusade in behalf of an inefficient and reactionary government. The argument . . . went like this: The United States had to make a choice between supporting temporarily a bad democratic government (democratic in form) and allowing an armed minority under Soviet direction to fasten a Communist dictatorship permanently upon Greece. . . .

Crucial to this analysis besides the dubious use of the term "democratic" was the assumption of "Soviet direction." As we have seen, the Soviets in fact were giving neither aid nor direction. A few months later they would vainly seek to persuade Yugoslavia to cut off the substantial aid which it was giving. "What do you think," Stalin exclaimed to the Yugoslav vice-premier in early 1948, "that Great Britain and the United States—the United States, the most powerful state in the world—will permit you to break their line of communication in the Mediterranean? Nonsense. And we have no navy. The uprising in Greece must be stopped, and as quickly as possible." Indeed, the Soviet attitude toward Greece conformed perfectly to the Stalinist pattern. Since the Greek guerrillas had taken action independent of the Red Army and Stalin's direction, the Kremlin viewed them as a nuisance and a possible threat to the diplomatic relations of the Soviet Union. Stalin saw them as potential clients of the Yugoslavs, whose claims to a role of independent political leadership in the Balkans he was already attempting to crush.[6]

The Barnet view has merit in that it illustrates an American idea that was dominant in 1947 and for long years thereafter; that is, that communism was monolithic, all of one variety, and all run from Moscow. Americans believed, and large numbers of us persist in it today, that all Communist nations and parties were puppets of the Kremlin, acting under its orders, and subject to minute control by Soviet leaders. If Barnet is correct, then the Yugoslavs, Albanians, and Bulgars, who had coveted Greek territory long before they even heard of communism, were acting in an independent manner for reasons of nationalism, not communism. American policy insisted on blaming the Soviet Union for all, however.

From the American point of view there was only one variety of communism, and even if we were to admit there might be more than one type, all were equally undesirable. Certain it is that if Yugoslav or Bulgarian Communists had gained control of Greece, the USSR would have moved to exploit the advantage.

Greece and Turkey could not be allowed to go Communist. Toward this end, President Truman stood before Congress and proclaimed the celebrated Truman Doctrine:

> I believe that it must be the policy of the United States to support free peoples who are resisting attempted subjugation by armed minorities or by outside pressures.
>
> I believe that we must assist free peoples to work out their own destinies in their own way.
>
> I believe that our help should be primarily through economic and financial aid which is essential to economic stability and orderly political processes.
>
> The world is not static, and the *status quo* is not sacred. But we cannot allow changes in the *status quo* in violation of the Charter of the United Nations by such methods as coercion, or by such subterfuges as political infiltration. In helping free and independent nations to maintain their freedom, the United States will be giving effect to the principles of the Charter of the United Nations. . . .
>
> Should we fail to aid Greece and Turkey in this fateful hour, the effect will be far-reaching to the West as well as to the East.
>
> We must take immediate and resolute action.[7]

President Truman then asked Congress to authorize the spending of $400 million for assistance to Greece and Turkey and to authorize the use of "American civilian and military personnel" in Greece and Turkey "at the request of those countries" to assist in reconstruction and to supervise the use of American assistance as well as to train Greeks and Turks in the handling of American materials.

It is more than interesting that virtually the same language Truman used could be and sometimes has been used to explain and justify American involvement in scores of nations, including Vietnam.

The Truman Doctrine was an avowed policy of containment. We would contain monolithic, imperialistic Soviet communism wherever it threatened to spread. We would use financial aid and military personnel for this purpose. In a word, the United States sought to contain the Soviet Union *militarily*.

The United States has traveled this long road ever since, but through time the doctrine has become somewhat distorted. Over the years we did not always await the request of the countries where we intervened or it came from officials of questionable authority. Not always did we act on behalf of free peoples to help them work out their own destinies. Most definitely our help has not been "primarily . . . economic and financial." All too often it has been military.

Professor Hans J. Morgenthau points to other changes in the Truman Doctrine over the years in his book, *A New Foreign Policy for the United States*. He maintains that the

. . . Truman Doctrine transformed a concrete interest of the United States in a geographically defined part of the world into a moral principle of worldwide validity, to be applied regardless of the limits of American interests and of American power.[8]

Yet, Morgenthau argues, the "globalism of the Truman Doctrine was not put to the test of actual performance." He adds:

It was the contrast between the sweeping generalities of the Truman Doctrine and the discriminating policies actually pursued by the Truman administration that was to haunt Messrs. Truman and Acheson in the years to come. Their foreign policies, especially in Asia, were judged by the standards of the Truman Doctrine and were found wanting.[9]

Professor Morgenthau is pointing out that the Truman administration did not apply the doctrine to China, North Korea, or North Vietnam, all of which went Communist in the Truman years. The doctrine was applied almost solely to Europe and even there little or no attempts were made to free the peoples of Eastern Europe.

Morgenthau sought to evaluate the performances of the next three presidents in applying the Truman Doctrine. The contrast between crusading pronouncements and actual policies continued and was even accentuated under President Eisenhower and his secretary of state, John Foster Dulles. Morgenthau said this was due "on one hand to his [Dulles's] propensity for grandiose announcements and, on the other, to his innate caution and President Eisenhower's common sense."

Under President Kennedy the gap between words and deeds "started to narrow." This was because Mr. Kennedy realized that communism was no longer the "spearhead of Russian imperialism," as he expressed it. The United States had to deal with different types of communism in emerging nations—such as Vietnam. Professor Morgenthau then described the Truman Doctrine under President Johnson:

> Under President Johnson, pronouncements and policies were, for the first time since the great transformation of American policy in 1947, very nearly in harmony. What President Johnson only implied, the Secretaries of State and Defense clearly stated: We are fighting in Vietnam in order to stop Communism throughout the world. And the President stated with similar clarity that "we do not propose to sit here in our rocking chair with our hands folded and let the Communists set up any government in the Western Hemisphere." What in the past we had said we were doing or would do but never did, we were now in the process of putting into practice: to stop the expansion of Communism on a global scale by force of arms.[10]

Almost twenty-two years elapsed between the formation of the Truman Doctrine and the end of the Johnson administration in 1969.

Clearly, when a person ponders the bloodshed, expense, and problems which have been the result of the Truman Doctrine over the years, he must inquire whether there were any possible alternatives. There were at least two which could have avoided the consequences of the doctrine, while aiding Greece and Turkey.

First, Mr. Truman and Mr. Acheson did not have to state the doctrine in such sweeping terms. The doctrine does not include the word "all," but it clearly implies that America would aid free peoples all over the world who sought freedom, fought subjugation, and/or wanted to work out their own destinies. If Truman and Acheson were being circumspect in avoiding the word "all," then later presidents tended to read the word into the doctrine.

Truman and Acheson did not need, as Professor Morgenthau suggests, to make the doctrine a "moral principle of world-wide validity."

The United States could have been more pragmatic. It saw the situation in Greece and Turkey as a threat to the vital interests of the United States. Acheson's exposition of the threat, quoted earlier, was perhaps valid. Greece and Turkey were the key to the domination of Europe, Asia, and Africa. President Truman could have cited the importance of Greece and Turkey to the United States, Europe, and the rest of the free world. He could have applied his doctrine to those two countries and let it go at that, thus making his doctrine an expression of the intent of the United States to defend its vital interests wherever affected in the world. Defending our vital interests may have been a less lofty promulgation than a moral crusade on behalf of free people, but it would have been a more accurate statement of what we had in mind: non-Communist governments in Greece and Turkey.

Second, even if for political, propaganda, or other reasons, the doctrine had to be placed on such a high moral level, it did not have to be carried out that way. We could have spoken loftily and acted pragmatically on behalf of national interests. As Professor Morgenthau suggests, Presidents Truman and Eisenhower more or less did that, while Presidents Kennedy and Johnson moved the deed closer to the word.

9

THE
MARSHALL
PLAN

THE MARSHALL PLAN followed quickly on the heels of
the Truman Doctrine as the second instrument of
American foreign policy designed to thwart Communist expansionism.

The plan is named for General of the Army George
Catlett Marshall, who perhaps served the United
States in more high-ranking capacities than any other
American in history. He was the Army Chief of Staff
during World War II, which means he was in charge
of the military conduct of the wars against Germany
and Japan. Both General Eisenhower in Europe and
General Douglas MacArthur in the Far East were sub-
ordinate to him. Later he made an extensive study of
the situation in postwar China and served as both secretary of state and secretary of defense for President

Truman. A quiet man, lacking the flair of either Eisenhower or MacArthur, he was widely respected for his intelligence, organizational ability, dedication, and patriotism.

On April 28, 1947, General Marshall, then secretary of state, returned from a six-week inspection trip to Europe. He told the nation in a radio address:

> . . . We were faced with immediate issues which vitally concerned the impoverished and suffering people of Europe who are crying for help, for coal, for food, and for most of the necessities of life, and the majority of whom are bitterly disposed toward the Germany that brought about this disastrous situation. . . .
>
> The recovery of Europe has been far slower than had been expected. Disintegrating forces are becoming evident. The patient is sinking while the doctors deliberate . . . action cannot await compromise through exhaustion.[1]

These words were true. Western Europe was in a state of economic collapse from the war. Peoples were exhausted and suffering. They lacked the means and often the will to rebuild their nations. The United States alone had the money to come to their aid. Simple human charity dictated that Americans reach out to help the homeless and suffering. There were other considerations. America's economic prosperity depended in large measure on foreign trade. A collapsed Europe would drag the United States down, too.

Finally, and perhaps most importantly, American leaders believed that the chaos of Europe was an open invitation for a Communist takeover. There were strong Communist parties in every Western nation, save England, with France and Italy being particularly threatened. It was an article of faith in American thinking that unemployment, poverty, hunger, and homelessness were the breeding grounds of communism. America must combat the spread of communism by economic aid.

General Marshall announced his plan for the economic recovery of Europe—quite to the surprise of Under Secretary Acheson—at a speech at the Harvard University Commencement, where the General received an honorary degree. The heart of the speech was as follows:

> 1. Our policy is directed not against any country or doctrine but against hunger, poverty, desperation, and chaos. Its purpose should be the revival of a working economy in the world so as to permit the emergence of political and social conditions in which free institutions can exist.
>
> 2. Such assistance, I am convinced, must not be on a piecemeal basis as various crises develop. Any assistance that this government may render in the future should provide a cure rather than a mere palliative.
>
> 3. Any government that is willing to assist in the task of recovery will find full cooperation, I am sure, on the part of the United States government. Any gov-

ernment which maneuvers to block the recovery of other countries cannot expect help from us. Furthermore, governments, political parties, or groups which seek to perpetuate human misery in order to profit therefrom politically or otherwise will encounter the opposition of the United States.[2]

The last paragraph, of course, was an open warning to the Soviet Union and the indigenous Communist parties of Europe.

The program for accomplishing the recovery of Europe, as put forth by Marshall, was a monument to diplomacy and restraint. He said:

It is already evident that, before the United States government can proceed much further in its efforts to alleviate the situation and help start the European world on its way to recovery, there must be some agreement among the countries of Europe as to the requirements of the situation and the part those countries themselves will take in order to give proper effect to whatever action might be undertaken by this government.

It would be neither fitting nor efficacious for this government to undertake to draw up unilaterally a program designed to place Europe on its feet economically.

This is the business of the Europeans.

The initiative, I think, must come from Europe.

This program should be a joint one, agreed to by a number of, if not all, European nations.

The role of this country should consist of friendly

aid in the drafting of a European program and of later
support of such a program so far as it may be practical
for us to do so.[3]

The Marshall Plan, known as the Economic Recovery Act (ERA), was adopted by Congress and about
$12 billion was funneled into Europe over a four-year
period. The plan has been considered an immense
success. The largesse of American dollars, which were
gifts and not loans, are credited with starting Europe
on its way to recovery, so much so that Europe is now
a major economic competitor of the United States.
The plan is also credited with saving Western Europe
from communism, whether or not that is entirely true.

The plan has been called a profound example of
"enlightened self-interest," for most of the money was
returned to America in the form of purchases. Thus
our own economy was stimulated by the money sent
overseas. Europe was helped and so were we.

So successful was the Marshall Plan that foreign aid
has been a fixture of American foreign policy ever
since. It has changed in scope and purpose. Aid is dispensed around the world, not just in Europe. Much of
the aid is in military weapons. It is no longer exclusively economic. The bill, according to President
Nixon in 1971, was $142 billion since World War II.

It is doubtful if that amount of money would have
been appropriated by the American Congress as an act
of charity. From its inception in 1948, and increas-

ingly over the years, the aid program has been billed as necessary to combat communism. Even with that rationale, foreign aid has remained highly unpopular in Congress. For many years the program has been slashed annually, and a succession of presidents have found passage difficult to attain. Finally, in 1972, the Senate defeated the foreign aid measure, a vote later rescinded under extreme pressure from President Nixon. Many political observers believe the days of the United States foreign aid program are numbered.[4]

If we return to the inception of the Marshall Plan, it becomes clear that the whole program was an accident of history. Needed and important it surely was, but it is amazing that it came to pass. The initial problem was that the Soviet Union and the other Iron Curtain countries of Eastern Europe wanted to be in on the aid program. The request put the United States into an instant bind. The aid had been offered on such a lofty, humanitarian plane that there was no reason to deny it to the Soviets, unless we wanted to admit the open anti-Communist nature of the plan, which we did not. Author Richard J. Walton has stated the problem succinctly:

> For more than two years Stalin had been seeking American aid to help reconstruct his devastated land, but the two nations had not been able to agree on terms. Could the United States now offer enormous sums to Western Europe and leave out Eastern Eu-

rope? If it did, wouldn't that prove what Stalin had been saying all along, that the United States wanted to divide Europe, control one half of it, while carrying out economic warfare against the other? [5]

America's dilemma was compounded by a simple political fact: if the Communist nations were to receive American economic aid, then the entire plan—which only squeaked through Congress as it was—would have no chance at all of being adopted by a Republican-controlled Congress. The United States had only weeks before announced the Truman Doctrine. How could it be expected to turn around and offer economic aid to the very Communist nations it was opposing? Besides, including the Soviet Union and its satellites would enormously increase the amount of aid.

Moscow quickly acted as though it intended to join the plan, much to America's apprehension.

Molotov met with Britain's foreign minister Ernest Bevan and France's Georges Bidault and all seemed to be going well, much to American misgivings. Then the meeting blew up. Acheson quoted Bevan's explanation:

> It seems that Molotov has a bump on his forehead which swells when he is under emotional strain. The matter was being debated and Molotov had raised relatively minor questions or objections at various points, when a telegram was handed to him. He turned pale and the bump on his forehead swelled.

After that, his attitude changed and he became much more harsh. . . . I suspect that Molotov must have thought that the instruction sent to him was stupid; in any case, the withdrawal of the Russians made operations much more simple.[6]

The telegram apparently bore Stalin's decision not to join the Marshall Plan, which must have occasioned a tremendous sigh of relief in Washington. Professor Ulam provides an exposition of Stalin's reasoning:

. . . the plan evidently was a gamble which Stalin could not take. The Soviet system could not afford disclosure of information about its economy, the standard of living of its people, or production norms. For one thing, except when it came to armaments and heavy industry, the government itself had no reliable data. As Khrushchev made clear after Stalin's death, figures relating to agricultural production were systematically falsified at the central as well as local levels, to such a degree that what might be described as statistical anarchy reigned, with neither the Central Committee nor the government really knowing the true state of affairs. But even taking all this into account, what has been revealed was a picture of weakness and misery that could only encourage an enemy and shock the most inveterate fellow traveler. Khrushchev alleged later that the government exported grain while conditions close to starvation prevailed in some areas, that in 1953 agricultural production in absolute as well as average terms was below that of 1913.

The broader problem of the morale of the Soviet

citizen and the effect on him of any kind of relationship with the West was equally insuperable. Here was
the regime instilling through plays, through speeches,
through a continuous din of propaganda the duty to
be vigilant, to be hostile to the bourgeois world. At
the same time, news would be spread of American billions pouring in to bolster the economy and raise the
standard of living. And what of the effect on the satellites? There was one thing which Stalin prized above
his country's economic strength, and that was his own
political power, and the plan which promised to advance some of his most cherished goals had to be
rejected.[7]

Stalin not only rejected the Marshall Plan, but prevented his satellite nations from joining. Strong Soviet
pressure was used to prevent Poland from accepting.
The Czechs did accept, whereupon its leaders were
summoned to Moscow and ordered to reverse the acceptance.

Ironically, Stalin may have unwittingly fostered the
aid program for Western Europe. Passage of the "give-
away" program (as critics dub it to this day) was far
from assured in the Republican Congress. Senator
Robert A. Taft of Ohio, the GOP majority leader, was
opposed to it. Debate was protracted and heated.
Then, in February 1948, while the debate was going
on, the Communists pulled a *coup d'état* in Czechoslovakia, a nation with which America had strong senti-

mental ties. America's old friend Jan Mazaryk was liquidated and the Czechoslovak nation slipped behind the Iron Curtain. After that the Marshall Plan was passed by Congress.

It is difficult to resist speculating a little on the might-have-beens of the Marshall Plan. Many historians maintain that Congress would never have appropriated aid funds for Communist nations.[8] But that is perhaps not wholly true. It did later for Communist Yugoslavia. Perhaps if the need for aid to the Soviet Union had been explained properly, Congress could have been persuaded to adopt it. Certainly if the Truman Doctrine, announced so shortly before, had been limited to Greece and Turkey and had been stated in less general anti-Communist terms, if we had been more willing to seek ways to cooperate and were less bent on hatred, then maybe . . . perhaps . . . we might be looking out on a different world.

One can only speculate also on what might have been if Stalin had been less suspicious and less a Marxist. If, wanting the aid, as he must have, he had sought compromise for half a loaf instead of all he wanted, Europe and the world would be a far different place today.

But Stalin was suspicious. He viewed the world through Marxist-Leninist principles. America just had to be imperialistic, attempting to gain with the dollar the influence it denied wanting by force of arms. He had a strong moral position. He could have addressed the world to cite Soviet sacrifices and challenged the United States to aid the suffering Soviet people. But apparently he could not admit Soviet weakness. Playing a strong game with a weak hand, he could not reveal the desperate straits of his own nation.

There are those who believe Stalin wanted the collapse of capitalism in Western Europe to pave the way for the inevitable Communist revolution.[9] Another view is that Stalin feared that the real goals of the Marshall Plan were to wean the Eastern European satellites away from the Soviet Union. The prosperous Western nations could become a powerful lure to the more impoverished and restricted Eastern Europeans. Uprising among the satellite peoples would perhaps inevitably follow.[10]

What have been the effects of the Marshall Plan? It was amazingly successful in promoting the recovery of Western Europe. Within two decades, European dependence upon the United States had been reversed and America was importing more from Europe than it sold—with serious effects on the American economy and the soundness of the dollar today.

The cooperation that the Marshall Plan more or less forced on the European nations led, if only indirectly, to formation of the Common Market in 1957,[11] which has become a major economic area rivaling the United States and the Soviet Union. The hope persists that these nations, so long at war with each other, will join to form something resembling the "United States of Europe" and become a powerful third force in the world.

Yet the Marshall Plan did contribute, as Stalin suspected it would, to the division of Europe into two rival economic and political blocs. There is a divided Europe today and only the slightest beginnings of cooperation between the Western and Eastern divisions. Other factors contributed to this, factors only distantly related to the Marshall Plan, but it was important to the creation of tensions and fears the continent has known ever since.

A final result of the Marshall Plan was its extension around the world. The United States has offered aid to underdeveloped nations, many of which had most unstable governments, some of which were anything but democratic, in a worldwide competition with the Soviets. The war in Vietnam is only one result of that.

It is at least questionable whether Marshall or Truman or Acheson or the leaders of Congress in 1947 ever envisioned the long commitment and the expense that they were beginning.

Was it necessary? In terms of European recovery the answer is a resounding yes. American aid was imperative. But that aid could have been given on purely humanitarian terms, a sort of international community chest. It did not have to be an instrument of anti-communism. The aid could have been urged upon the Russians, if only on the same basis that we aided that nation following the First World War.

But that is pie-in-the-sky. In the climate of opinion in America following World War II, foreign aid to the Russian people would have been construed as aiding and abetting an enemy. Congress probably would not have accepted it. But why did we and the Soviets have to see each other as enemies? Could we not have remained simply competitors? We will pursue answers to these questions, but first we must consider some other important elements of America's postwar foreign policy.

10

THE
KOREAN
WAR

Observe good faith and justice toward all nations; cultivate peace and harmony with all. . . . The nation which indulges toward another an habitual hatred or an habitual fondness is in some degree a slave.

THAT IS A quotation from George Washington's Farewell Address to America, which was the core of American foreign policy until after World War II. One other sentence from Washington's address needs to be cited: " 'Tis our true policy to steer clear of permanent alliances, with any portion of the foreign world." [1]

This advice, long honored in America, fell into ill-repute and disuse following World War II. Washington was speaking in the days when America's ocean frontiers were nearly impassable barriers. They certainly isolated the United States from the quarrels of Europe and Asia. But World War II technology changed all that with the long-distance airplane, then the jet, then the intercontinental ballistic missiles and satellites. Americans great and small came to believe that America had to become internationalist. What happened in Europe, Asia, Africa, or South America intimately affected America. Few if any people disagreed with this sentiment.

Our determination to become an internationalist nation, never again to resign our role in world affairs, led us to contravene all of Washington's advice. We hardly cultivated peace and harmony with Communist nations. Instead we viewed them with implacable enmity.

And we chose to become involved in a skein of permanent alliances. The mere listing of them is impressive:

1. We fostered the North Atlantic Treaty Organization (NATO) on April 4, 1949, joining with most of the nations of Western Europe in agreeing that an attack on any one of the European nations was an attack upon all. We pledged ourselves to a continuing military commitment in Europe.

2. We joined the Southeast Asia Treaty Organization (SEATO) on September 8, 1954, calling for collective defense with Australia, France, New Zealand, Pakistan, the Philippines, Thailand, and Britain.

3. In September 1951, we joined with Australia and

New Zealand in the ANZUS treaty, agreeing that any attack in the Pacific area against one member was an attack against all.

4. In 1947, the Rio Treaty was signed agreeing to "reciprocal assistance" between the United States and Latin American nations.

Many treaties and agreements were signed with individual nations, until by the mid-1960s the United States was firmly committed to more than forty-three nations, as calculated by the Symington subcommittee of the Senate Foreign Relations Committee. It is a statement of fact, not a witticism, that we as a nation said farewell to Washington's address.

All of these alliances were in pursuit of the policy of containment. We persisted in the latter half of the 1940s in the opinion that the Soviet Union was a military giant, possessed of some sort of invincible land armada that could envelop the world if ever unleashed —and Americans greatly feared it would be unleashed. When the Russians exploded the atomic bomb in 1949, we became petrified with fear of an atomic holocaust.

It is a known fact today that the Soviet Union was a paper giant, abysmally weak while maintaining a front of superstrength. The simple exigencies of the Soviet economy had forced the Russians to engage in a massive demobilization. By 1948, the Soviet army was down to less than three million men, a minimal amount considering the farflung demands on the Soviet garrison.

There were many signs of Soviet weakness. The

USSR never did fully ensnare Finland. The Finns pursued a pro-Soviet policy and went to great pains to maintain amicable yet independent relationships with their behemoth neighbor. More evidence was the independent line taken by Marshal Tito in Yugoslavia. Tito remained a dedicated Communist, but he refused to follow the Russian policies. Stalin threatened: "I will shake my little finger—and there will be no more Tito." [2] But Tito remained. Clearly communism was not a monolithic exercise dictated from Moscow. Tragically, it took Americans many years to realize this.

Perhaps the greatest evidence of Russian weakness in the face of American strength came in 1948 with the Soviet blockade of Berlin. The pre-war German capital which lay in the Soviet zone but was divided into British, American, French, and Russian zones, was blockaded by the Russians on June 24 in response to the issuance of new West German currency in the Allied zones.

Two days later, President Truman announced that the United States would provision West Berlin by an airlift. It seemed an idle boast considering the tremendous demands of West Berliners for food and, particularly, coal for electricity and heat. But the United States scraped together every available transport plane. Many were brought from as far away as the Caribbean and the United States. The flights droned on day and night. The West Berliners, while on short rations and not always warm, survived. The airlift to Berlin, which lasted for 324 days, is considered a miracle of modern aviation.

The airlift was seen as evidence of American determination to defend its commitments. Most historians consider it a monumental blunder by Stalin. It demonstrated American strength and Russian weakness. It called Stalin's bluff and showed that the Soviet Union would not go to war to back up its strategies. The blockade and airlift drew West Berlin and all of West Germany closer to the West. More importantly, it hardened Soviet-American relations. The cold war became colder.

Relations reached the frigid point on June 25, 1950, when Communist North Korea, well equipped with Soviet arms, invaded South Korea. The Korean War was the major event of the Truman administration and, until the war in Vietnam, the most important event in postwar history.

The Korean peninsula is a thumb of China extending toward Japan. The Korean people had long been subjugated, first by the Chinese, then the Japanese. At the end of World War II, Korea had been divided along the 38th parallel into the North, occupied by Russian troops, and the South, occupied by Americans. North Korea had been turned into a Communist state with a powerful army. South Korea had been of little importance to the United States. Some aid was dispensed and efforts made to create a democratic form of government. By 1950 most American troops and advisors had been withdrawn. The South Korean military force was extremely weak. It was no match for the North Koreans bent on unifying the peninsula under Communist rule.

Professor Stoessinger does not discuss the Korean War in any detail, but it seems to be further evidence for his concept that imperception has played a major role in the cold war. Imperception on both sides led to miscalculations with tragic results.

The chain of events leading to the Korean War was somewhat complicated. The postwar civil war between Chiang Kai-shek and Communist Mao Tse-tung ended in the fall of 1949. Chiang fled with remnants of his forces to the island of Formosa off the mainland, and Mao proclaimed the Communist People's Republic of China on October 1.

Two results probably seemed likely to Stalin. If the Soviet leader had difficulty controlling the breakaway ideology of Tito in Yugoslavia, he could anticipate far greater problems with Mao. The Chinese leader was a strong-minded man. He had carried on his revolution for decades, fighting both the Japanese and the Nationalist Chinese at various times. He had won it with little aid from the Soviet Union. Moreover, he espoused a brand of communism considerably different from that in Russia. He considered himself equal to if not superior to Stalin as the oracle of true communism. Frictions between the Chinese and Russian Communists were inevitable, as later events proved.

Stalin perhaps expected, or at least feared, that the United States might exploit these ideological differences, make some overtures to the Red Chinese, perhaps in the form of loans, and thus dilute Moscow's influence. But the Americans did not. We were obsessed with the monolithic nature of communism and saw the Chinese revolution as Moscow-inspired and Mao as a mere puppet of Stalin. More than two decades would pass before an American president (Nixon) began to exploit Russian-Chinese differences and to make overtures to the Red Chinese.

The second possibility in the Soviet mind in 1949 was that the United States would re-arm Chiang's army and have it launch an attack on the mainland with American naval and air support. The United States did not, because of its dislike for an Asian war, the relative weakness of Chiang, and fear that the Russians would enter and launch World War III. The fact that the Sino-Soviet treaty applied only against an attack from Japan on China made no impression in Washington.

A third possibility in the Russian mind was that the United States might retaliate to the communization of China by re-arming Japan and unleashing it against the Soviet Union at Vladivostok and Sakhalin. Again, in this event, the Sino-Soviet treaty would not apply. At the very least Stalin must have expected the United States to reverse its policy in Japan and re-arm it as a counterthreat to Communist expansion in the Far East.[3]

But America did none of these, perhaps leading to the conclusion in Moscow that the United States could be pushed even further in Korea.

To Stalin's mind, allowing or even ordering the North Koreans to attack the South seemed to offer distinct advantages, in Professor Ulam's view, which are worth enumerating.

1. The North Koreans should win an easy victory in the South, thus creating another bit of Communist territory.

2. The victory would shove the Americans entirely off the mainland. The conquest of Korea would pose a military threat to Japan, the major American bastion in Asia.

3. The communization of all of Korea would greatly encourage Japan's native Communists and have a profound effect on the non-Communist Japanese government. Perhaps all American forces would be withdrawn, leaving Japan defenseless. If Japan became Communist, it would give the Kremlin a second power-base in the Far East, one to be played off against the troublesome Mao. Or, if the Americans beefed up their defenses in Japan, this would surely weaken American military commitments in Europe.

4. Finally, the invasion of Korea was a means by which Soviet soldiers could be kept in China. Under the terms of the Sino-Soviet treaty, the Russians were to leave no later than 1952.

Stalin was probably considerably surprised by the

American decision to fight for South Korea. The United States had acquiesced in the loss of China. It had made no effort to re-arm Japan. It had ignored a series of warnings and minor skirmishes indicating that the Korean invasion was imminent. As late as June 12, two weeks before the attack, Acheson had declared that South Korea was beyond the American defense perimeter. Then, within days of the invasion, President Truman committed American naval, air, and then ground forces to repel the invasion. Stalin must have reacted with consternation at such irrational American conduct.

The best indication of Stalin's surprise is the fact that Soviet representatives had temporarily walked out of the United Nations somewhat earlier. Stalin had long successfully used the Soviet veto in the UN Security Council to block international actions. With the Russians absent from the UN, the United States was able to turn the conflict into a United Nations war against an aggressor. This put the war on a higher moral plane, which pleased Americans, even though it was largely an American war.

Americans also possessed a series of imperceptions and miscalculations which perhaps prolonged the war. Professor Ulam offers a provocative analysis:

There is a strong presumption that the Soviets might have been tempted to call off the whole thing. This would have been relatively easy: having chas-

tised the "invaders," the North would virtuously return where they came from. From this temptation the
Soviets were probably rescued by the perceptible apprehension and disarray which lay behind the seemingly resolute American and UN action.[4]

At the beginning, the United States was shown to be
militarily weak. In all of the Pacific we could not scrape
up a single combat-ready division to throw into the
breach in South Korea. The troops we did send were
poorly trained and soft from occupation duty in Japan.
Their courage stemmed the tide of the North Korean
advance near the tip of the peninsula, the so-called
Pusan perimeter.

American military unpreparedness must have been
an overwhelming temptation for Stalin. How wonderful for him if the Americans could be driven into the
sea. The early lessons of Korea were never again lost on
Americans. Military preparedness became an American gospel. We no longer could count on the atomic
bomb to prevent war. Furthermore, a generation of
Americans came to believe that the Russians could
only understand and react to strong military force. If
they saw military weakness they would exploit it.
These became covenants of American foreign policy.

The apprehension and disarray also included American fears of an atomic confrontation with the Soviets.
As Professor Ulam put it, "No sane person could doubt
the ultimate Soviet responsibility for the attack." [5] Yet
neither President Truman nor the United Nations re-

acted with a strong ultimatum to the Russians to call off the attack. Rather, the United States sent a note of record asking the Soviets to disavow any responsibility for the attack. This the Russians did gladly. When the United States asked the Russians to use their influence with the North Koreans to call off the attack, the Russians said they had no power to interfere. North Korea was, after all, a sovereign state.

Clearly, American leaders believed their own scare stories about the great strength of the Russian military machine and believed also that the Soviets were bent on world conquest through armed aggression. Militarily weak ourselves, we reacted with fear and took elaborate steps to mollify the USSR.

The United States entered the war for the highest moral reasons. We viewed the North Korean invasion, and properly so, as a clear-cut act of aggression. With World War II fresh in our minds, we were not about to let aggression go unpunished, as we had prior to the great war. More, under the Truman Doctrine, we were pledged to defend small nations. Few at the time or since have done anything but applaud President Truman's decision to intervene.[6] When we were able to get United Nations sponsorship, our moral position was complete.

There is no need here for more than a brief resumé of the war, which went on for more than three years. The United States aroused itself to a war footing and, after containing the North Koreans at the Pusan perimeter, began to push northward. The invasion collapsed when General MacArthur achieved one of his most brilliant military tactics, the landing of troops at Inchon, far up the coast of South Korea. With the North Koreans in danger of being trapped, they hastily retreated and South Korea was emptied of the aggressors as rapidly as they had arrived.

Then came a fateful American decision. Heady with military success and imprisoned by our old World War II idea of unconditional surrender, American and UN forces plunged into North Korea in the hope of trapping the remnants of the North Korean army and then uniting all of Korea under South Korean aegis.

MacArthur, overwhelmed by a feeling of invincible genius following Inchon, made blunder upon blunder. Ignoring the appeals of his field commanders, he dispatched the thin American forces all over North Korea in reckless, headlong advances. He, as well as Washington, ignored Chinese threats as mere bluffs. Worse, when American troops skirmished with Chinese troops in North Korea, MacArthur disbelieved the reports. He ordered his troops northward and some reached the Yalu River bordering China.

On November 26, 1951, Chinese forces struck. American troops reeled backward, only courageous rear-guard actions preventing an out-an-out rout. American forces retreated halfway down through South Korea before holding. Then, in a long grueling struggle, United Nations forces finally pushed the Chinese and North Koreans back to approximately the 38th parallel, where the war stalemated. Negotiations to end the war were begun in 1951 and dragged on before an armistice was finally signed on July 27, 1953.

Several points are important about the effects of the war on Soviet-American relations. First, Congress was never asked to declare war. President Truman labeled it a "police action." It was thus an important precedent for later presidents to engage American troops in combat without congressional approval.

Second, Mr. Truman wanted to fight only a limited war, one that would not enlarge beyond Korea to involve the Soviet Union. The refusal to formally declare war was to that purpose, as was his decision not to bomb China or attack it directly.

Third, the war came to enrage many Americans because Mr. Truman did not fight to win it, rather than settling for the stalemate. Much of this controversy centered on General MacArthur who wanted to unleash Chiang's forces to attack China, send American bombers over China, and blockade the Chinese coast. Ultimately, President Truman relieved the wartime hero of his command. This kicked off a gigantic furor. To this day, many Americans of conservative views believe MacArthur was right and that America should have used all its military power to crush North Korea and China.[7]

Not the least effect of the war was our long antipathy toward the People's Republic of China. We hoisted our star over Chiang on Formosa and neglected all efforts at rapprochement with the Red Chinese. Even as the antagonism between China and the Soviet Union worsened, we failed until 1972 to seek any advantage from it.

The Korean War was a gross miscalculation on all sides. The United States became totally convinced of the aggressive nature of communism. Our policy of containment, through both alliances and military preparedness, was pursued diligently by every president after Truman. Virtually all efforts at negotiation or compromise were denounced. America and the USSR, the free and the Communist worlds, became two armed camps, each manning the ramparts, each menacing and distrusting the other.

11

THE BATTLE
FOR EUROPE

ALL THROUGH THE Korean War, President Truman
and Secretary of State Acheson recognized that the
main battleground was in Europe. If there was to be
a direct military confrontation between the United
States and the Soviet Union, it was most likely to occur
there.

Both nations feared the intentions of the other. The
United States feared that the Soviet Union would try
to grab Western European lands by military force. The
Soviet Union feared that Western Europe was being
armed for an eventual attack on the USSR. As a result,
both sides began diplomatic and military initiatives to
protect themselves.

The focus of the East-West confrontation in Europe
was Germany, which straddled the Iron Curtain at its

center. To understand the unique position of Germany in the cold war, we must backtrack very briefly to the end of World War II. At that time Germany had been considered the greatest possible threat to the peace of the world, both East and West. Twice in a generation Germany had been fought and Europe, Germany included, lay wasted. A major concern of world leaders was to prevent Germany from ever dragging the world into war again.

There were those who wanted a Carthaginian peace, with Germany prevented from ever rising again. In America the principal advocate was Henry Morgenthau, Roosevelt's secretary of the treasury. The so-called Morgenthau plan envisaged the destruction of Germany's heavy and medium industry; the main industrial areas of the Ruhr and the Saar and Silesia would be detached from Germany, to be partitioned into two separate states, their inhabitants relegated to mainly agricultural pursuits and their standard of living kept well below the rest of Europe's.[1]

Such schemes never really received serious consideration, for Roosevelt and Churchill realized there could be no economic recovery in Europe without German participation.

At Yalta, Roosevelt, Churchill, and Stalin agreed to divide Germany into American, British, French, and Russian zones of occupation, based in the main upon where the various Allied troops were. At the Potsdam conference in 1945, Truman, Attlee, and Stalin reached a more detailed agreement on Germany. Chief authority in each of the occupation zones was to be transferred to the respective military commanders and to a four-way Allied Control Council for matters affecting the whole of Germany. The Nazi party was to be outlawed, and steps taken to abolish the Nazi ideology. Germany was to be disarmed and prevented from ever again becoming a military power. Democratic ideals, including elected representative government, were to be fostered. The German economy was to be decentralized and monopolies broken up. Agriculture was to be encouraged.

Such plans, to whatever extent they were practical, were beached on the shoals of Soviet-American distrust. The origins of the cold war lay not in Korea but in Germany.

As we have seen, NATO was formed on April 4, 1949. NATO was a reaction to the American and European perception that the Soviet Union posed a dire military threat to Western Europe. Europe had the umbrella of American planes carrying the big bomb, but Europeans must be prepared to defend themselves against the hordes of Red Army soldiers. Americans would participate in the NATO force and provide aid for the European partners. Most of all, the military force had to be created before the Russian attack so as to be a deterrent to it.

As originally formed, NATO had no German participation. It is known that many American leaders of government believed German participation would ultimately be necessary. Professor Stoessinger states that Acheson held such a private belief and military chieftains did so openly. A Western defense plan had been drawn in the Pentagon in 1949 in which German participation was considered essential. But the Americans could never have sold such a scheme to the other NATO partners, who feared a revitalized Germany as much or more than the USSR.

This attitude was undermined by Stalin's gross miscalculation in Korea. The open aggression there was seen in Washington, as well as other NATO capitals, as an opening gambit—it was feared that Soviet aggression in Europe would be next. Korea thus "precipitated the first and only serious attempt to create the forces . . . for withstanding a Soviet attack in Europe." [2]

In September 1950, with American forces hard-pressed to contain the Korean invasion, the American, British, and French foreign ministers met in New York. The United States agreed to name an American as the Supreme Commander of an integrated NATO command and to increase its troops in Europe—two matters the Europeans considered very urgent. In return, the United States asked that ten or twelve German divisions be included in the NATO forces.

The proposal caught Europeans in the middle between their fears of both Germany and the Soviet

Union. In the end they worked out a plan for the European Defense Community (EDC), a sort of super-national European military force. This scheme lingered on for more than four years, before being wrecked by the French decision not to participate. The foreign ministers did, however, agree in principle to German military participation in NATO and the relaxation of restrictions on German industrial production.

To Americans, all this was simply self-defense against the Soviet menace. To the Soviets it was something else. When the United States ended the state of war with Germany without the consent of the Soviet Union, it had clearly violated the Potsdam agreement. Furthermore, American motives were transparent to the Soviets: we wanted to use Western Germany to further "the aspirations of the USA ruling circles for world supremacy." [3] When the United States lifted the limits on German steel production, it meant that the steel would be used to aid the "Western Powers' military strategic war tasks." [4] The Soviets found it impossible to believe that these moves had a purely defensive purpose. They demanded a return to the terms of the Potsdam agreement as a demonstration of Western good faith toward the USSR.

The USSR suggested a conference to discuss such a return but the United States, as Stoessinger puts it, "convinced of *Soviet* bad faith" (his emphasis), opposed it unless general problems of East-West tensions were included in the agenda. "The Soviets took the rejection as the expected endorsement of their original conviction," Stoessinger wrote.

American policies continued regardless of Soviet disapproval. In December 1950, the NATO Council agreed to German participation in an integrated European military force. On July 9, 1951, the United States, Britain, and France formally ended the war with Germany. In May 1952, agreement was reached between the three Western powers and West Germany (the Federal Republic of Germany) ending the occupation and abolishing the high commission.

The Russians were enraged, calling them the actions of "imperialist warmongers." The Soviet Union launched a series of diplomatic moves to stop these developments, but all failed. The United States wanted free all-German elections as a condition for German reunification. The USSR could not agree to this for fear of losing East Germany to the West. It replied with a plan for an all-German Constituent Council with equal representation from each Germany. This council was to prepare a provisional government for a reunited Germany. The United States rejected this scheme for if only a few West Germans voted with the East Germans, America would be unable to control the council. Next the Russians offered free elections under the council's aegis in which "all

democratic parties and organizations" were to participate. This plan was rejected in Washington in the
belief that Russian definitions of democratic political
parties would be far removed from American definitions.

Clearly, the United States and the USSR had
reached a point of total distrust of each other's motives. Both believed the other was maneuvering to
absorb the whole of a reunified Germany into its
sphere of influence. Lacking any trust in each other's
intentions, it became impossible to devise any diplomatic formula to resolve the impasse.

Soviet diplomatic initiatives were unabated. The
USSR accepted an American demand for a guarantee
of democratic rights to all Germans. It even offered to
allow Germany an independent armed force sufficient
for its national defense. Finally, it accepted the principle of free all-German elections subject to control by
a four-power commission. But, in return, Germany
was to pledge not to join any alliance against any nation which had fought Hitler. This, of course, meant
NATO.

All these were turned down by the United States
and its European allies. American distrust, in Stoessinger's words, was now "too firmly entrenched." We
saw the Soviet overtures as ploys to drag all of Germany under Communist influence, or as plans to so
weaken NATO that it would not be effective.

The Soviets then came up with a new proposal, which Professor Stoessinger describes most effectively:

On March 31, 1954, the USSR announced that it intended to apply for membership in NATO. The Soviets argued that if NATO were indeed a true collective security pact, and not a closed alliance directed specifically against the Soviet Union, the Western powers could have no excuse for excluding the USSR. If, on the other hand, they did in fact deny the Soviet application, their real intentions would be unmasked.

The American reaction was one of stunned disbelief, although among Western diplomats in Moscow, there were some who held that the Soviets were actually serious. A new realization among the Soviet leaders of the perils of atomic warfare, these observers maintained, had caused a genuine reassessment of the world situation, a clearer grasp of the dangers of war in a world of nuclear weapons, and a determination to avoid such a holocaust.

The State Department, however, declared that it had "no evidence" that Moscow was "sincere" in seeking an end to the cold war. The Soviet Union, it said, was trying instead to recover from its failure . . . to "undermine Western security."

The United States thus rejected the Soviet bid out of hand. When criticized by other NATO nations for acting precipitously and without consulting its allies, the United States defended its behavior by stating that it had "wanted to avoid any impression that the proposals were getting the slightest consideration." [5]

What makes all this the more amazing is that a great

deal had happened in the world to indicate a new climate or at least an opportunity for some start toward trust and cooperation. By 1954, the Korean War had ended. Stalin had died in May 1953, and a new generation of leaders occupied the Kremlin. Truman and Acheson had been replaced by Eisenhower and John Foster Dulles. Eisenhower had had some friendly relations with the Russians during the war. But none of this seemed to have the least effect on cold war tensions.

The remaining diplomatic developments can be quickly summarized. When the plan for a European Defense Community was killed in Paris in 1954, the United States quickly pressed for the precise thing the Soviets wanted least, the admission to NATO of an independent West Germany, free of all postwar restraints. The Russians repeated their offer for free all-German elections, if plans to remilitarize Germany were abandoned. The offer was repeated again. Stoessinger comments:

> It was too late, however. German reunification was now relegated to second place in American priorities. Overriding all else was the imperative of NATO defense. First, the Soviets' urging that a conference to discuss their proposal be convened in the fall of 1954 was taken not as a sign of anxiety but as proof of insincerity, for as Secretary of State Dulles remarked, "the Soviets knew very well that such high-level conferences could not be prepared on such short notice." [6] Molotov accordingly proposed a delay—on

the condition that . . . [Germany not be admitted to NATO] . . . until the conference had taken place. The United States saw this condition as the real objective: to paralyze Western defense.

The USSR, for its part, saw the United States' *rejection* [his emphasis] as its real objective—to let nothing prevent the Americans from reviving a Wehrmacht. . . .[7]

Full sovereignty was granted to West Germany on May 5, 1955 and it was admitted to NATO on May 9. The Soviet Union reacted by forming its satellites into a Warsaw Pact group and rearming East Germany.

The results of all this can be assessed from the hindsight of seventeen years. There are those who maintain that the Truman-Acheson, Eisenhower-Dulles policies were acts of brilliance, forging an Atlantic alliance which thwarted Soviet expansion into Europe. Perhaps, but there are other results. Germany remains divided to this day with little hope for unification. NATO still exists, but it is far less important to America than it was. France virtually withdrew from it, leaving it greatly weakened. Moreover, most Europeans have long ceased to consider Russian invasion a very likely happenstance. They are far more interested in trading with the Russians. Ironically, the Germans have given every indication that their military spirit is dead. They want most of all to make money and lead peaceful lives rather than attempt to conquer the world. Thus the fears of both sides in the 1950s seem to have been groundless.

Professor Stoessinger's thesis that such events as the remilitarization and division of Germany were rooted in mutual Soviet-American misperceptions of each other's intent has a high degree of validity. But it does not explain all. Politics, on both sides of the Iron Curtain, seems also to have played a role.

12

THE STATIC YEARS: 1955–1970

By 1955, THE main elements of American foreign policy toward communism had been formed. They were simply continued by a succession of presidents.

First, there was unrelenting enmity. American leaders talked of peace, of wanting it and searching for it, but with few exceptions chances for improved relations were drowned in distrust and antagonism. The political climate in the United States remained such that no president, however popular, could undertake a policy of rapprochement with the Soviet Union or China. Because we had said for so long, and continued to say, that communism was such an unmitigated evil, that no Communist leader would negotiate in good faith or keep his word if he did, that Americans had a moral, even holy obligation to protect freedom around the world from communism, that the Communists were bent on world conquest, there was no way American leaders could meet the Russians even halfway in the direction of peace.

The second element of our policy was containment. The Communist bloc—USSR, the Eastern European satellites, and China—was ringed by alliances and armaments. The United States set up military bases around the world. We developed a fleet of long-range bombers carrying nuclear weapons, then long-range ballistic missiles. These could be fired from nuclear submarines continually operating at sea or from land bases ringing the Communist world.

Our foreign policy toward the non-Communist world—which included many neutral "third world" nations, such as India, the African nations, and perhaps Yugoslavia—was largely aimed at supporting containment. Long after the intercontinental missiles made many of our overseas bases obsolete, we continued to maintain them. Our desire for these bases led us to support any stable government that was non-Communist, even if it was a dictatorship. Somehow we believed that these bases, the security they offered the host countries, and the money flowing from these bases into the local economies would bolster these nations in their anti-communism.

Military supremacy, not just preparedness, was the third element of American policy. The United States must be more powerful than the Soviet Union both in quality and quantity of weapons. Secretaries of defense, generals, and admirals merely had to trek to the Capitol and report to Congress the Soviet Union's increased strength—or perhaps only its possibly increased strength at some future date—to gain a nearly blank military check from an eager Congress. Indeed, the legislative branch from time to time appropriated funds for military weapons which presidents and the armed forces did not want.

Fourth, we were ready and willing to use this military force wherever we deemed freedom to be threatened. We used it in Formosa to strengthen the Nationalist Chinese, in Guatemala, Lebanon, Cuba, The Dominican Republic, and throughout Southeast Asia, and waved a big stick in various other places. In addition, as noted, we offered billions of dollars annually in military and economic aid to nations to strengthen their anti-communism.

These were the four major elements of American foreign policy. There were only minor differences as administrations came and went. The Eisenhower administration, with its foreign policy largely fashioned by John Foster Dulles, relied more heavily on the nuclear threat to enforce containment. The word "brinksmanship" [1] was coined during Dulles's tenure. It meant he was willing to go to the brink of an atomic holocaust to thwart Red imperialism. Kennedy quickly altered this by placing greater emphasis on conventional military forces so that the United States would be better prepared to fight small, limited wars. The Pentagon was delighted to receive more money for conventional weapons as well as nuclear ones. Despite the brinksmanship, the Eisenhower administration was more cautious in committing American forces. No major conflicts broke out during the eight Eisenhower years, the conflict in Vietnam being rather minor at the time. Kennedy and particularly Johnson demonstrated a far greater willingness to use American pilots, sailors, and soldiers to combat Communist threats.

Soviet foreign policy seemed to undergo significant changes during the period. After Stalin's death in 1953, and an inevitable power struggle, a form of collective leadership came to exist. Nikita Khrushchev became Communist Party leader and Nicolai Bulganin premier. That lasted for a while, then Khrushchev emerged as sole leader, with Bulganin, Molotov, and other political opponents being relegated to minor posts. Then, in a bloodless coup in 1964, Khrushchev was ousted into retirement and collective leadership again returned in the form of party leader Leonid Brezhnev and Premier Alexei N. Kosygin.

One of Khrushchev's main accomplishments was the de-Stalinization of the Soviet Union. In a famous speech in 1956, he listed the brutality and terror of the Stalin years, as well as the mistakes of government by "personality cult." Americans were delighted by the confirmation of what they had believed all along about Stalin, the embarrassment of Communist parties in the

United States and other nations, and the tearing down of Stalin statues, the expunging of him from history books, and the removal of his body from the Lenin crypt in Red Square. None of this created any significant changes in American policies, even when the anti-Stalin campaign worsened relations between Moscow and Peking and caused friction with the Eastern European satellites.

Khrushchev, joined at first by Bulganin, embarked on what seemed to be a new foreign policy. Both were portly, seemingly jolly men. Khrushchev was the closest thing to an American-style politician the Soviet Union has produced. Together or separately Khrushchev and Bulganin became world travelers, visiting such places as India, Burma, Afghanistan, Yugoslavia, various European capitals, Britain, and even the United States, where Khrushchev greeted Hollywood stars, petted farm animals, and admired American corn crops—all amid vast publicity.

The aim of the tours was to demonstrate that Soviet leaders, now that Stalin was gone, had become more reasonable and civilized. By being cheerful and outgoing, Khrushchev hoped to demonstrate to the world that there was no longer much need for NATO defenses and the American policy of containment.

Some sort of thaw did seem to occur in the cold war. A few American tourists were admitted to the Soviet Union and Khrushchev seemed genuinely interested in gaining American expertise to improve the near desperate state of Soviet agriculture.[2] Some increase in trade occurred. There were exchanges of scholars, athletes, and a variety of artists.

A new term came out of Moscow, "peaceful coexistence." The idea was that the two great economic and ideological systems need not be totally incompatible. There need not be war or even enmity. They could live side-by-side in the world and engage in friendly competition to see which was the superior.

American leaders joined in some of these new international antics. American presidents, beginning with Eisenhower, embarked on tours through the world, too. They intended to shore up American alliances and show American determination against communism through personal diplomacy.

Meetings with the new Soviet leaders became a vogue. A big-four summit[3] conference in Geneva, Switzerland, in July 1955 conjured up great hopes throughout the world, including the United States, that the cold war might end. But virtually nothing of substance happened. The conference, like the tours, was largely a public relations exercise with the leaders reading prepared speeches under the eyes of television cameras. Indeed, Eisenhower had promised before going that this was not to be another Yalta and that no secret agreements would be made. That in effect meant *no* agreements would be reached.

Another summit was to be held in Paris in May 1960, but it was wrecked when the Soviets shot down an American U-2 spy plane and Eisenhower was forced to admit such spy flights had been going on regularly. In the hoopla of Soviet denouncements of America, Eisenhower's planned trip to Moscow was canceled.

But summitry remained in vogue. Kennedy met Khrushchev at Vienna, Johnson conferred with Kosygin at Glassboro, New Jersey, and Nixon in 1972 made trips to both Peking and Moscow. All of these were claimed to be of great value and all vastly improved the popularity of the incumbent president. Presumably, the Soviet leaders involved recorded similar gains in popularity among the Russian people. Yet nothing of substance resulted from the Johnson meeting. Kennedy's visit to Vienna may indeed have been harmful, as we shall see. The Nixon visits have occurred too recently for any assessment of their results, although he did negotiate treaties limiting the arms race and calling for joint efforts in space exploration and pollution control.

American leaders perceived the Khrushchev activities as an effort to seed disunity among our allies. They saw the jolly-seeming Russian as seeking to weaken the resolve of our friends by showing himself and thus by implication all Communists as friendly, decent, genuinely interested in peace and thereby not any military or ideological threat to the rest of the world.

The Russian policy was undermined by several events. The satellite countries seemed to mistake Khrushchev's joviality for an invitation to seek greater independence from Moscow. There were riots and attempted uprisings in East Germany and Poland. The most serious was in Hungary where young "freedom fighters" took up arms and actually overthrew the existing government. The brief revolt was brutally crushed by Red Army tanks in October 1956, and bleeding Hungary was pulled back behind the Iron Curtain.

Unrest remained unabated among the satellites. Yugoslavia maintained its non-satellite status and even won the regard of the United States. Rumania maintained a somewhat independent stance in foreign affairs, even entertaining President Nixon on one of his world tours, as did Poland. Albania embraced the Chinese brand of communism and the Soviets did little about it. Poland reshuffled its government in the face of strikes by workers. But tragedy befell Czechoslovakia in 1968. A more liberal Communist regime under Premier Alexander Dubcek was crushed, amid some violence, by Soviet tanks. These events, spanning more than a decade, convinced doubters that the true nature of communism was still brutal, imperialistic, and anti-freedom. The Soviet style may have turned to smiles and sweet reasonableness, but underneath was the same old totalitarian iron fist.

If Americans were not fooled by the public relations gambits of the Soviets, neither did we understand the importance of the Eastern European nations to the Soviets in the 1960s any more than we had in 1945. The

Russians felt their security depended on the satellites perhaps more than ever, with a rearmed West Germany in one direction and growing troubles with the People's Republic of China in the other. The always strained relations between Moscow and Peking had drifted into open hostility and finally armed clashes along their far-flung border. By 1970, the Soviets were perhaps perceiving the Chinese as a greater threat to them than the Americans. The Chinese, on the other hand, feared the Soviets more than they feared the United States.

From 1945 through 1970, there were really no substantive changes in American foreign policy toward the Soviet Union. Harry Truman, retired in Independence, Missouri, must have been unable to see any significant differences in the actions of his successors from those he had taken.

American foreign policy remained stable, despite the great changes that had occurred in the world. Vast growth had taken place in technology. Electronics came on with a rush, leading to immense improvements in communications, television, data processing, computers, minute radios and listening devices, and so forth. Electronics was the basis for unparalleled improvements in weaponry, more sophisticated nuclear weapons, incredibly accurate bombs and missiles, jet aircraft breaking the sound barrier, and much, much more. The missile age came, with each nation having the capability to pulverize the other within minutes.

Russia launched the first earth satellite, the Sputnik, in 1957, and ushered in the space age leading to men on the moon and probes to nearby planets.

There were significant political changes. Leaders came and went in both the United States and the USSR, bringing new styles and fresh opportunities for peace. Social changes gripped the world with the death of colonialism. Scores of new nations were formed in Africa, Asia, and in the Pacific. Nationalism, race, and emerging nations gave the world a whole new set of problems.

Economically, the world of 1970 bore little resemblance to that of the 1940s. Europe revived and united into the Common Market. It became an economic bloc rivaling the United States and the Soviet Union. People spoke of the "miracle" of West Germany and Japan, both of which became economic and industrial powers. Britain, France, then China developed atomic weapons, and both Israel and India claim they have the capacity to do so. China, still woefully weak, came on nonetheless as a third superpower with potential to surpass perhaps even the United States in time.

All this may be summarized by saying that the United States was no longer the overwhelmingly dominant power in the world, militarily, economically, or politically. By the 1970s, we had become a debtor nation in terms of world trade. We purchased far more from other countries than we sold them. The dollar, for years the foundation of all Free World currencies, had fallen in value until even the United States was seeking payment in foreign currencies rather than its own dollars. At home we had severe economic problems of inflation and unemployment. This does not mean that the United States had become weaker; the rest of the world had become stronger. We had become first among equals.

Yet our foreign policy of unrelenting enmity to communism (and willingness to go to war against it), containment, and military supremacy remained without significant change after Truman. (There may be significant changes in the Nixon administration, which we will take up shortly.)

We must now assess some of the results of our tenacious policies toward communism and the Soviet Union.

13

A TIME
OF CRISES

Let every nation know, whether it wishes us well or ill, that we shall pay any price, bear any burden, meet any hardship, support any friend, oppose any foe to assure the survival and the success of liberty.

**—John F. Kennedy
Inaugural Address**

THOSE WORDS UTTERED by President Kennedy, in January 1961, were an expression of the American commitment to oppose the spread of communism anywhere in the world. We most certainly did carry a great burden, endure hardships, and pay a high price in terms of lives, money, and loss of national resources in pursuing this policy.

From 1955 to 1970, the United States and the Soviet

Union, democracy and communism, confronted each other all over the world. Crisis followed upon crisis—in Europe, the Middle East, Africa, Latin America, several parts of Asia. Threats were made, missiles were rattled, troops deployed, guns fired, and lives and homes lost. American soldiers and sailors were often involved and not uncommonly Soviet personnel were in an area of conflict. But most of the combat occurred among Communist and anti-Communist factions in a particular area. Thus, many of the crises had the characteristics of civil wars in which the United States and the USSR intervened.

No mistake should be made. Such incidents as an uprising in Guatemala, an aborted invasion of Cuba, open warfare in the Middle East, India, or Southeast Asia were confrontations between the Soviet Union and the United States. With precious few exceptions, the two superpowers were on opposite sides, arming and supporting economically and politically the faction they favored.

There is no need here to give a full accounting of all these crises. But we should study some of them in search of a few of the characteristics of the Soviet-American confrontation in the 1950s and 1960s and the results attained.

The first observable characteristic is that both the Soviet Union and the United States sought to achieve domination over a particular country or geographic area by peaceful means. Both superpowers freely dispensed ideological support and immense sums in economic aid to those countries which seemed to be wavering between communism and democracy. There were outright grants of money, loans, favorable trading agreements. Personnel were often sent to provide technical training or assist in solving local problems. The money was intended to insure the friendship and loyalty of the recipient. The personnel were often a means of creating either democratic or Communist institutions in the host countries.

In many instances the fate of a particular cold war battle was decided by a checkbook. Perhaps the most celebrated example was that of Egypt, or the United Arab Republic, as it is now called. In 1952, the regime of corrupt King Farouk was overthrown by a group of military officers led by Gamal Abdel Nasser. Truman and Acheson began a generally friendly and helpful policy toward the new regime, but when Eisenhower and Dulles took office in 1953 they, in the words of historian Morison, handled the situation "with incredible gaucherie and stupidity."

As a gesture of friendship to Nasser, the United States persuaded Britain to remove its garrison which guarded the internationally operated Suez Canal. This left Nasser in complete military control of the vital waterway. Then, in 1955, Nasser sought funds from the United States to build the giant Aswan Dam on the Nile River. It would provide massive amounts of electricity and open large acreage to irrigation and cultivation. The cost was expected to be between $1.3 and $2 billion. The United States and Britain joined in an offer of loans to finance the project.

Nasser was dissatisfied with the terms and negotiations began. Meanwhile, Secretary Dulles became disenchanted with Nasser. Historian Sidney Warren explained the reasons:

> Nasser engaged in a series of actions which seemed deliberately intended to antagonize the West. He purchased arms from Czechoslovakia in defiance of an agreement that arms be kept out of the Middle East, stepped up the commando raids against Israel, aided the Algerian rebels against France, and used his controlled press and radio to laud the Soviets while excoriating the democracies. Finally, when Dulles heard inspired rumors that Nasser had been offered a twenty-year loan by the Soviet Union, he withdrew the offer of assistance. Britain followed suit.[1]

The repercussions of the cancellation of the loan offer came swiftly and have been long-lasting. Nasser retaliated by nationalizing or seizing the Canal and appropriating all its toll receipts for his national treasury. Britain and France became alarmed that Nasser would cut off their vital oil supplies which were shipped via the Canal. They began negotiations with an obdurate Nasser, while secretly planning a military strike to take back the waterway.

The strike occurred in October 1956. Israel invaded the Sinai Desert toward the east bank of the Suez.

Britain and France bombed Egyptian airfields and landed troops. The Soviet Union immediately branded the British-French-Israeli actions as "imperialist" and colonial aggression. The USSR promised to come to the aid of the United Arab Republic unless there was an immediate cease-fire. It hinted at dropping atomic bombs on England and France. President Eisenhower, who knew well in advance of the British-French invasion plans, announced his "amazed stupefaction" at their actions. He denounced the invasion and joined the Soviet Union demanding a cease-fire. Denied American aid, faced with Soviet threats, Britain, France, and Israel backed down and removed their forces.

The results: the Suez Canal remained under Nasser's control. American influence in the Arab states of the Middle East was reduced to nil. The Soviet Union, having offered economic aid and then promised military assistance in an hour of need, became the paramount influence in the United Arab Republic and other Arab states.

There is no point in speculating on what might have happened had the United States loaned money for the Aswan Dam. The Israeli-Arab conflict made the Middle East a tinderbox at best. But it is safe to say that the precipitous cancellation of the loan offer threw away much of America's opportunity for influence in the Arab lands, while greatly enhancing that of the Soviet Union.

The Suez crisis also illustrates a couple of other difficulties that arose as the United States and the Soviet Union sought to compete economically for the less-developed nations of the world. Nasser clearly was attempting to play off the two superpowers against each other to receive the greatest possible amount of aid. It was a tactic used by leaders of Ghana, Indonesia, and various other countries. A dangerous game it was, for the United States has expected as a price for its aid that recipients would be at least neutral in the cold war and preferably openly anti-Communist.

The United States Congress, which has been a great deal less than enthusiastic about foreign aid for many years, has a tendency to cut off aid to those countries which it considers hostile to America. As a result, several nations have come under Soviet influence and found it difficult to extricate themselves. Nasser was not a Communist, nor is his successor Sadat by any meaning of the word. Yet dependent on Soviet aid, they both found it difficult to maintain their nation's independence in the face of Soviet demands. In 1972, Sadat took the step of ordering all Soviet personnel out of the United Arab Republic, lest they run the country rather than he. Similar actions occurred in Ghana and elsewhere.

A more serious problem illustrated by the Suez crisis is that the economic aid from both the United States and the Soviet Union seemed inevitably to involve military aid. Weapons were introduced and the purely economic or ideological competition between the superpowers escalated into a military confrontation. It has happened all over the world until a fairly predictable pattern has resulted.

The Middle East is a good example. There was an attempt or at least a hope in the late 1940s and early 1950s that the area could remain largely disarmed. The hatred of the Arabs for the Israelis was so great that conflict was simply unavoidable. With the Arab states determined to drive the Israelis into the sea and the Israelis committed to defending their historic homeland, the introduction of sophisticated modern weapons was an invitation to chaos. Weapons were introduced, however. The adversaries made some of their own, and they bought more from willing suppliers. The French were particularly eager salesmen. As one side or the other proved to be or threatened to be militarily superior, still more weapons were purchased to maintain the balance of power.

Both the United States and the Soviet Union were soon dragged into the arms race. The United States supplied Israel and the Soviet Union the United Arab Republic. The arms were a sure way to guarantee continued influence, for the antagonists needed to buy replacement weapons and parts which could come only from the original manufacturers. Personnel had to be assigned to give instructions in the use of the weapons. Thus, a conflict between the Israelis and the Arabs became a possible confrontation between the Russians

and the Americans, for weapons and personnel of both
were involved.

The pattern has been repeated in scores of nations.
India buys weapons from the Soviet Union and the
United States supplies Pakistan. The North Koreans
and North Vietnamese have Russian or Chinese weapons, the South Koreans and South Vietnamese American arms. We supply the Nationalist Chinese on Formosa.

The supplying of weapons poses potentially lethal
problems. The Symington subcommittee of the Senate
Foreign Relations Committee reported, in December
1970, that the United States had agreed, in return for
permission to open a communications base, to equip a
40,000-man Ethiopian army. The new military force
was considered a threat by the government of Somali,
which borders on Ethiopia. The Somalis promptly
beefed up their army with weapons provided by the
Soviet Union. The subcommittee observed that a big
power confrontation was thus created where none had
existed before.

The second characteristic of the various worldwide
crises of the cold war is that when conflict did occur
both the United States and the Soviet Union tried to
let other nationalities do the fighting and dying. The
Soviet Union has been a good bit more successful in
this than the United States. Soviet troops have been
used to suppress insurrections in its Eastern European
satellites and in a border clash with the People's Re-

public of China, but they have not been directly involved in any of the other conflicts of the last quarter century. In contrast, American troops have been used in Korea, Vietnam, Lebanon, and the Dominican Republic. There were threats of American military power in other places, including the Congo, Jordan, and Cuba.

The principal means by which both superpowers have let others do the fighting and dying is by sometimes arming and supporting insurgent groups, sometimes the established government the insurgents sought to overthrow. With native soldiers firing the weapons, the big powers have confronted each other in all the corners of the world.

Again there was a pattern. An insurgent group would be established, claiming to be either Communist or anti-Communist. The group might be indigenous to the area, having sprung from local political or economic dissatisfactions. Or, the group might be fomented and financed by agents of either the United States or the Soviet Union. In either case, the insurgents soon received money, weapons, and technical advice from one of the big powers. Some sort of coup, uprising, or civil war occurred. The opposite superpower, which usually supported the established government, aided its friends.

One of the earlier examples of this pattern—still not widely known in the United States—occurred in Guatemala in 1953–54. Its constitutionally elected presi-

dent, Jacobo Arbenz Guzmán, a professional army officer, had turned Communist after taking office. In all
probability he switched to communism more from political necessity than from conviction. He wanted to do
something about Guatemala's feudal land system in
which 2 percent of the population owned 70 percent of
the land. The largest owner was the American-owned
United Fruit Company. It farmed bananas on several
hundred square miles of land. The country was marked
by serfdom, poverty, and high illiteracy.

Arbenz was simply not strong enough politically to
push through his reforms. He was opposed by the large
landowners. The United Fruit Company was angered
when he nationalized 225,000 acres of its holdings. Despite Arbenz's military background, he was disliked by
Guatemala's military leaders. Somewhat surprisingly,
Arbenz did not have a large following among the nation's peasants and workers whom he sought to help.
They disliked him for his bad temper and high-pitched
voice.

Arbenz's main support came from the Communists,
who had been operating for years among the workers
on banana and coffee plantations. Arbenz embraced
the local Communists and then the Soviet Union,
which responded with aid, agents, advice, propaganda,
and shipment of Czechoslovakian weapons.

The situation was intolerable to the Eisenhower administration. The Central American nation was just
a short plane ride south of the United States and it was

even closer to the vital Panama Canal. The Soviet Union could not be allowed to gain a foothold in the Western Hemisphere.

Meetings were held at the highest levels in Washington, with President Eisenhower and Secretary of State Dulles participating. It was decided to overthrow the Arbenz regime with a revolution. This task was assigned to the Central Intelligence Agency (CIA) whose head was Allen Dulles, brother of the secretary of state.

Plans for the insurrection were developed by Frank G. Wisner, a deputy CIA director. Assigned to carry them out in Guatemala was John Emil Peurifoy, United States ambassador to that country.

Every revolution needs a leader. The man chosen by the CIA (after its first choice had refused the job) was Colonel Carlos Castillo-Armas, a long-time opponent of Arbenz. He had led an unsuccessful revolt in 1950 and been imprisoned, only to tunnel his way to freedom. He was believed to have the dash and popularity to lead a successful revolution.

Castillo-Armas quickly recruited a band of followers. The CIA would supply them with weapons. But where were they to be trained? Hardly on Guatemalan soil. The problem was solved when American diplomats, under CIA guidance, prevailed on neighboring Nicaragua and Honduras to harbor the revolutionaries. Neither government wanted a Communist neighbor.

Castillo-Armas set up headquarters in Tegucigalpa, the capital of Honduras, and training began in Nicaragua on the estate of President Anastasio Somoza on the island of Momotombito in Lake Managua. Americans arrived to instruct the Guatemalans in revolutionary warfare. The CIA even supplied an air force of sorts— a handful of vintage World War II fighter planes— and troop transports. American civilian pilots were recruited, notably a swashbuckling adventurer named Jerry Fred DeLarm.

In January 1954 Arbenz denounced the revolutionaries with considerable accuracy, naming names and bases and sources of supply. The United States State Department declined comment, saying, "We will not give the story a dignity it doesn't deserve."

With its satellite now endangered, the Soviet Union stepped up its aid. On May 15, a ship bearing two thousand tons of arms docked at Guatemala, having eluded American vessels blockading the coast. The United States reacted by openly airlifting guns and ammunition to Nicaragua.

Castillo-Armas led his "army of liberation" from Honduras into Guatemala on June 18. Leading the rather ragtag band of revolutionaries was a battered station wagon. The invasion proceeded six miles to the Guatemalan town of Esquipulas, where Castillo-Armas encamped. He had no taste for fighting. He was determined to wait out the downfall of Arbenz and let the CIA air force do battle for him.

The events that followed had an almost comic-opera cast. DeLarm and other pilots bombed the country's main seaport at San José, as well as other targets, and dropped propaganda leaflets on the capital, Guatemala City. Arbenz protested that he was being invaded, but the State Department replied that in so far as it knew Guatemala was the scene of a revolt of the people against the government.

The raids were kept up largely unopposed. The defection of the leader of the government air force had a demoralizing effect on Arbenz, and he thereafter distrusted his own pilots so much that he grounded all his planes.

Then, disaster struck for the CIA. Its tiny air force was soon wiped out by a series of accidents and antiaircraft fire. Meetings were held in Washington in an atmosphere of crisis. If the United States supplied new planes, it was feared we would be open to a charge of aggression. The problem was solved by having the government of Nicaragua buy the planes with money secretly supplied by the CIA.

On June 24, the air raids were resumed. Three days later Arbenz announced his resignation in favor of Colonel Carlos Enrique Diaz, chief of the Guatemalan armed forces. Diaz promptly shocked the Americans by announcing his determination to continue the fight until the invaders were driven out of the country. Ambassador Peurifoy reportedly strapped on a .45 caliber weapon and began maneuvering to oust Diaz. DeLarm came to his rescue, bombing the government radio station and other installations. Diaz surrendered to a less militant army junta chosen by Peurifoy. Ultimately elections were held and Castillo-Armas elected president.

Some years later, the CIA attempted to overthrow the Communist government of Cuba by similar means, but the results were disastrous. With the approval of the Eisenhower administration, about fifteen hundred Cuban refugees were recruited and equipped by the CIA. They were trained in Central America for an invasion of Cuba at Golfo de Dochinos, the Bay of Pigs. According to the plan, the invaders were to be welcomed, harbored, and supported by Cubans who would revolt against Castro.

The invasion did not take place until April 1961, three months after John F. Kennedy became president. He did not take personal charge of the operation but, rather, leaned heavily on the advice of the CIA and his military chieftains. The invasion was a failure. The force was neither large enough nor sufficiently well armed to be successful on its own. It was met by the Cuban military forces rather than by revolting Cubans. The invaders' only chance for success lay in strong United States air and naval support. Kennedy was unwilling to supply this, for it would make the United States guilty of aggression against Cuba. The invaders were captured. Cuba and the Soviet Union scored an important propaganda victory, while American prestige fell in the Western Hemisphere.

The Soviet Union has attempted many similar types

of insurrections, winning some and losing others. The United States has customarily opposed the Soviet attempts. Over the years, the two superpowers have expended a considerable amount of money, equipment, and ingenuity on these enterprises, but with exceptions to be noted below, the operations have not cost many lives. A relatively small number of spies, agents, diplomats, mercenaries, and adventurers have been lost by both sides, but American and Soviet troops have, for the most part, not been used.

The exceptions to this pattern form the third characteristic of the cold war crises of the 1950s and 1960s. The United States—not the Soviet Union—has used its own troops in foreign lands when it felt local anti-Communist forces were in danger of losing.

President Truman did this in the Korean War. President Eisenhower dispatched American forces to Lebanon in 1958 for essentially the same reason, although the situation was considerably different. Nasser's United Arab Republic had proven to be decidedly expansionist after the Suez crisis. Syria was absorbed and Nasser masterminded a coup in Iraq, leading to the killing of King Faisal and his family. Similar pressures were being brought on both Lebanon and Jordan. In danger of being toppled, the Lebanese government asked for and received American troops. They went ashore near Beirut without incident and there was no fighting. Britain met a similar request from Jordan. The integrity of both nations was preserved, although

American influence did not last very long in Lebanon.

President Johnson sent American troops to the Dominican Republic in April 1965, in what was a very controversial action. Duly elected President Juan Bosch was overthrown in September 1963 by a military group led by Reid Cabral. The situation continued to be unstable, and on April 24, 1965 fighting broke out between Bosch and Cabral forces. Four days later, American troops began landing. President Johnson reacted to reports from the American embassy that the Bosch forces were controlled by Communists and that they were winning. There were also reports that Americans on the island were in danger and that many atrocities had occurred. Reporters on the scene, however, could identify few Communists in the Bosch forces and found little evidence of atrocities or danger to Americans.

The interventions in Lebanon and the Dominican Republic were rather painless for the United States. The troops arrived and were effective in maintaining anti-Communist governments. The soldiers were soon withdrawn with few if any casualties. This was not the case in Korea or in Vietnam, where American troops engaged in heavy fighting and brought the United States to a war footing. Clearly, there is a considerable risk of war in the dispatch of American troops to foreign lands.

The fourth characteristic of the cold war crises has been the elaborate efforts taken by the United States and the Soviet Union to avoid military conflict between each other. The atomic holocaust that might result could easily destroy both nations.

The United States and presumably the Soviet Union operate a so-called fail-safe system, which is aimed at guaranteeing that no atomic weapon or missiles or aircraft carrying them can be fired accidentally. The American system is reported to leave the final decision in the use of such weapons up to the president, thus preventing one of the great threats of the arms race.

A telephone "hot line" has been established between Washington and Moscow to provide instant communication at moments of crisis. The line was reportedly used in the Arab-Israeli Six Day War in 1967 to prevent any accidental engagements between American and Soviet forces that were in the area. Presumably the telephone line has been used in other crises.

Each nation tries to avoid military actions in those areas where the other is known to be operating. Russian personnel have pretty much stayed out of Vietnam. In 1972 when President Nixon ordered the mining of the North Vietnamese harbor at Haiphong, he gave the Soviet Union three days to remove any of its ships that might be in the area. In the Middle East, the United States has apparently cautioned the Israelis to be careful in attacking any bases where Russian personnel were quartered. When contact has been unavoidable, military personnel were not used. Gary Powers, the pilot of the U-2 spy plane shot down over the Soviet

Union in 1960, was a civilian. So were DeLarm and the other Americans in Guatemala. The Soviet ships spying off the American coasts are fishing vessels.

Technology has enabled both nations to reduce the risks of military engagements, while permitting each to maintain high levels of surveillance of the other. In the 1950s there were several incidents in which American bombers accidentally strayed over the Soviet borders while on reconnaissance flights. Such tasks have now been largely taken over by earth-orbiting satellites.

Diplomatically, the two nations may not have cooperated to relieve tensions and avoid confrontations, yet restraint was shown in avoiding ultimatums and putting adversaries in positions of impasse which could lead to war. Both sides often expressed a willingness to negotiate, even if those negotiations were fruitless. Both frequently took international issues to the United Nations, which became largely a debating society. At least a pretense was made of listening to the views of the other and of neutral nations, if only to immediately rebut them. And both nations possessed the veto over UN actions which might go against the interests of any big powers or compel them to war to preserve their vital interests. In many of the world trouble spots, such as the Middle East, India-Pakistan, even Vietnam in the early days, both the United States and the USSR tended to accept international United Nations commissions designed to supervise the tenuous peace.

Yet the risks of war between the United States and the Soviet Union, if only through accident or miscalculation, were great during all these years. Both nations seemed many times to teeter on the rim of the nuclear abyss. Perhaps the greatest risk was the Cuban missile crisis of 1962. It also serves to illustrate the restraint both powers used in the end to avoid the final confrontation.

The Cuban missile crisis was a product of miscalculation. As such, it differed little from the other major confrontations of the cold war. As we have seen, Stalin miscalculated American resolve and caused the Korean War, and the United States prolonged it by miscalculating the intentions of the Chinese to enter it. As we will see in the next chapter, the war in Vietnam is a product of American miscalculations of its own powers. The miscalculation in Cuba was Khrushchev's incorrect conception of President Kennedy. The Soviet leader had misread Kennedy's conduct during the Bay of Pigs fiasco as evidence of weakness and indecisiveness. When the two men met in Vienna, Khrushchev apparently formed an impression that Kennedy was a pleasant, handsome, but weak man. Khrushchev and the other Soviet leaders surrendered to the temptation to exploit what they believed to be a flaw in the character of the American chief executive.

The result was the missile crisis of October 1962. As the Kennedy people expressed it, there was an "eyeball to eyeball" confrontation until Khrushchev blinked. This, of course, is remarkably similar to the brinksmanship of John Foster Dulles.

United States aerial surveillance caught the Soviets building missile bases in Cuba. Pilots saw ships at sea, headed for Cuba with long "silo-like" objects on their decks.

The Kennedy administration went into action. A special group was organized to deal with the crisis. Secret meetings were held in the dead of night. All information was gathered and conferees calculated all their options. A Kennedy speech to the nation was drafted, redrafted, and then polished. The missiles posed an intolerable threat to the United States. They had to be gotten out. No greater crisis had ever existed in American history. Atomic war was imminent.

The President, having made his decision that the missiles had to be removed, faced the following ways of accomplishing the task: an invasion of Cuba or an air strike, both of which would have removed the missiles but probably killed a lot of Russians; a blockade to prevent more missiles from arriving, along with an ultimatum to Khrushchev to remove those already there; or negotiation. We could easily trade our no longer important missiles in Turkey, say, for the removal of the Cuban missiles.

Kennedy rejected the invasion or air strike as too great a risk of war. The Soviets might feel compelled to retaliate if their personnel were killed. He rejected negotiation, for it demonstrated weakness and invited the Soviets to take other such actions in the hope of negotiating the United States out of its containment policy. He chose the blockade and ultimatum. It also offered the Russians a face-saving way out. Kennedy tersely addressed the nation. Foreign diplomats were informed. Windows on American embassies were taped against breakage. Khrushchev backed down and the missiles were removed. Virtue triumphed. Another crisis passed.

In general, Americans think of the Cuban missile crisis as an ennobling moment of courage in our history. But there are growing criticisms. Richard J. Walton, writing in 1972, said this of Kennedy's handling of the crisis:

> It is difficult to escape the conclusion that . . . he deliberately built up the crisis, possibly to influence the elections, possibly to force the showdown with Khrushchev that he had long thought might be necessary. He gambled when there were too many unpredictable things that could have gone fatally wrong. His public and surprise ultimatum to Khrushchev risked nuclear war and, because it was wholly unnecessary, risked it to a degree beyond forgiveness. Clearly, however great his reluctance, Kennedy did seem, on the evidence of his friends, more willing than Khrushchev to take that last fatal step. One can only wonder, if their roles had been reversed, if Kennedy would have been able to accept public humiliation at the cost of avoiding nuclear war.[2]

Some questions are in order. The Russians weren't doing anything to us that we weren't doing to them. What would have been our reaction had the Russians forced an eyeball-to-eyeball confrontation over our Turkish missile bases? What hope had we that they would not someday do so? Was the crisis so serious that action had to be taken at once? Was it a true crisis or did we merely consider it a crisis? Were Kennedy and his advisors over-reacting to a previous display of weakness? Was Kennedy slavishly following postwar policies and attitudes set by a former president old enough to be his father? Did he, instead of merely resolving another confrontation, muff an opportunity for a courageous lessening of cold war tensions? Instead of innovating, did he react on the basis of attitudes which had consumed Americans and their substance for a half century?

Probably no one will ever have the answers to these questions, but it is my opinion that such questions should have been asked at the time and, for the most part, were not.

What were the results of all these years of crisis? What did the United States accomplish with all of its sacrifice in behalf of a foreign policy of consistent and wholehearted opposition to communism? The scorecard is still not tallied and probably will not be for many years, but already it shows both victories and defeats. A victory in Guatemala and the Dominican Republic, a loss in Cuba. A win in the Cuban missile crisis, a loss of American influence in the Arab nations. A gain in Ghana and Indonesia with the toppling of Communist-leaning leaders, a setback with the election of an avowed Marxist in Chile. A gain in friendlier relations with Yugoslavia and Rumania, a loss in growing Soviet influence in India.

The tally can go on and in the years ahead it will doubtless change to gains where there were losses and vice versa. But the tally already shows that the United States, for all its efforts, was far from successful in its pursuit of the policy of containment. It may be argued that without the policy, Soviet gains would have been far greater. Perhaps, but then it could also be argued that some other, less militant policy might also have been more effective.

The biggest item on the scoresheet of American foreign policy from Truman to Nixon is the Vietnam War. It is this we take up next.

14

THE SHOALS
OF VIETNAM

*The myth that the Chief Executive is the fount of
all wisdom in foreign affairs today lies shattered on
the shoals of Vietnam.*
—**Senator Frank Church of Idaho**

MORE THAN THE MYTH of presidential wisdom is shattered in Vietnam, if "shattered" means that large numbers of Americans are asking questions about recent history and searching for new directions. The Truman foreign policies seem to be changing as a result of Vietnam, although the direction of change is far from evident.

The war in Vietnam has been the ultimate crisis for Americans, the most involved and costliest of the succession of crises which the nation has faced since 1947.

It is the direct result of our foreign policy steadfastly followed since Harry Truman. While we have fought Vietnamese and not Russians, it remains, as in the other crises, a conflict with communism and the Soviet Union, which has supplied ideological, economic, and military support for the Vietnamese.

So much has been written about the Vietnam War[1] that there is no need here for a detailed account. United States involvement in its longest and least liked war is a classic case of creeping commitment. It is also a study in how a foreign policy designed for the problems of an earlier era can be tragic if continued too long.

War in Vietnam has been going on since December 19, 1946, when fighting began between the French, who had been pre-war colonial masters of Vietnam, and the Communist North Vietnamese, the strongest of the various groups in Vietnam. The French tried to rally the non-Communist forces to their side and in July 1949 set up the nation of South Vietnam. The United States recognized this new state in February 1950, and President Truman sent a thirty-five man military group to advise its troops on the use of American weapons. This was the beginning of American involvement. In December 1950, the United States signed a mutual defense assistance agreement with South Vietnam, and in September 1951 began to provide direct economic aid to the non-Communist nation.

The problem of Vietnam dragged on largely unnoticed in the United States. At that time it is doubtful if any but geography enthusiasts could have said where Vietnam was. Americans were more involved in the Soviet threat to Europe and the Korean War.

In 1954, after the French were defeated at the battle of Dien Bien Phu, an attempt was made to settle the Vietnam problem at a conference in Geneva, Switzerland, attended by France, Britain, the Soviet Union, the United States, North and South Vietnam, People's Republic of China, and Laos and Cambodia, two nations bordering Vietnam. France and North Vietnam agreed to partition the nation along the 17th parallel, ban new troops and bases in the area, hold reunification elections in July 1956, and create an International Control Commission of India, Canada, and Poland to supervise the agreement. The United States and South Vietnam did not sign the agreement. As matters developed, the Geneva agreement must rank as one of the least meaningful in the history of the world.

After the French defeat, the United States inherited the defense of the South Vietnamese nation. It was threatened not only by North Vietnam, but also by a large Communist insurgency group within its own territory, the Viet Cong, who were supplied by the North Vietnamese, Red Chinese, and Russians.

President Eisenhower began a slow stepping up of the military and economic aid to South Vietnam. The fighting continued and the first American military advisors were injured on October 22, 1957. The first

United States combat deaths occurred on July 8, 1959.

By May 5, 1960, near the end of the Eisenhower administration, American military personnel in South Vietnam numbered 685. President Kennedy accelerated the procession of GIs to the area until there were about fifteen thousand in Vietnam in December 1963, just after his assassination. This build-up followed statements by Mr. Kennedy that the United States was prepared to help South Vietnam "preserve its independence."

The late President admitted, according to his biographers, that the growth of the American commitment to South Vietnam occurred rather by default during his administration. Kennedy had not been particularly interested in Vietnam.[2] It was still a minor item in our global commitments to contain communism. Our dispatch of men, materials, and other aid to South Vietnam might be characterized as a sort of reflex action. Since 1947 we had been committed to opposing communism everywhere in the world. The North Vietnamese and insurgent Viet Cong, which threatened the integrity of South Vietnam, were clearly Communist; therefore we opposed them.

Comparisons with the Korean situation were easy to make. Both areas, formerly united in the past, had been victims of Japanese occupation. Both had been divided into Communist and democratic halves. It was clear that the North Vietnamese, if they had not actually invaded the South, were vigorously supplying the Viet

Cong. Americans saw the differences between Korea and Vietnam as only a matter of style. Where the North Koreans had openly invaded with their troops, the North Vietnamese were performing aggression by subversion and aid to Communist insurgents. In the American view, the results were the same. And the United States had to act to thwart these new methods as it had the "naked aggression" in Korea.

But there were differences between Korea and Vietnam. There was a question whether South Vietnam was a viable nation. It had deep religious and ethnic rifts among its people. There was a pronounced elitist ruling class through which a strong streak of corruption ran. There were grave doubts as to how much of the people's loyalty the South Vietnamese rulers could command. There was considerable evidence that a succession of South Vietnamese governments were being propped up by American aid. The strongest, best organized element in the South was the Viet Cong, and, had communism not been an issue, the United States would have looked upon the conflict solely as a civil war, stayed out of it, and recognized the winner. The issue for debate throughout the 1960s and into the 1970s is whether the United States *should* have looked upon the conflict as a civil war, communism notwithstanding, and stayed out of it.

Whatever we should have done, the United States greatly increased its commitment in Vietnam, beginning in 1964. The true facts are not yet known in full.

But, judging by the Pentagon Papers[3], American naval vessels apparently were aiding South Vietnamese troops in raids on North Vietnamese islands in the Gulf of Tonkin. On August 2–4, 1964, North Vietnamese vessels attacked American destroyers in the Gulf, believing them to be part of the raiding flotilla. The vessels actually were conducting spying activities.

The attacks were presented to Congress and the American people by the Johnson administration as acts similar to piracy or "naked aggression" on American ships making an innocent passage on the high seas. On August 7, Congress adopted the so-called Gulf of Tonkin Resolution authorizing President Johnson to "take all necessary measures to repel any armed attack against the forces of the United States and to prevent further aggression."

The United States began open bombing of North Vietnam in February 1965. Ever increasing numbers of American troops were sent to Vietnam until they numbered over half a million. American involvement in the war came to exceed even that in Korea, as did American casualties. It became a largely American war against the North Vietnamese, who were supplied by the Chinese and Russians.

The American aim in the beginning was to establish a viable, non-Communist government in South Vietnam. We had a choice of two methods to accomplish this. We could win a military victory, crushing the Viet Cong and North Vietnamese, or we could force these two groups to negotiate terms favorable to the United States and South Vietnam.

Both methods posed extreme difficulties. The nature of the war and the terrain were such that the United States could win a clear-cut military victory only by greatly increasing our armed forces in Vietnam. We would have to occupy the whole of both the North and South for a prolonged period, and as conquerors impose our will. Such an action might have involved the United States in another land war with China and perhaps even the USSR. It was a commitment no American president was prepared to take, for the American people would not have supported him.

The negotiated settlement, which was the true purpose of American policy, turned out to be extremely elusive. The North Vietnamese proved to be a most dedicated, Spartan lot, who simply could not be bombed to the conference table. They demonstrated a remarkable capacity to endure heavy punishment on battlefields and from the air, to keep on fighting, to ask for and accept more punishment, and then to insist upon terms of negotiation entirely favorable to their cause: the United States should get out of Vietnam.

To Americans, the entire situation by 1969 had become inconceivable and totally frustrating. Here was the world's greatest military power pitted against one of the most backward nations on earth, which had had more bombs dropped on it than had been visited on either Japan or Germany in all of World War II. And

North Vietnam was not only not surrendering, it was still attacking on occasion. At the very least, the North Vietnamese were suggesting that the United States surrender, not they.

Few issues in American history have so consumed Americans as the war in Vietnam. It divided Americans into "hawks" and "doves." Protests against the war, based upon our moral position in it, began on college campuses and grew until hundreds of thousands of people were demonstrating at one time. Riots, shootings, and other forms of violence were spawned. Americans turned on other Americans in unrelenting violence, with the war as a root cause. The high price of the war for Americans was not the tens of thousands of lives, the billions of dollars wasted, and the economic problems which resulted, but the divisiveness. We had not been so disunited since the Civil War.

President Johnson, although he disputes it, was probably driven from office over the Vietnam issue. Richard Nixon was elected president in 1968 on a pledge to end the war "with honor." He began this task by enlarging it into Cambodia and Laos. He sought to "Vietnamize" the war by withdrawing American troops, while arming the South Vietnamese to assume the ground fighting. By late 1972, most of the American ground combat forces had been withdrawn.

But the war went on. The North Vietnamese spread into Cambodia and Laos. In the summer of 1972 they mounted a major offensive into the South as if they had never sustained a casualty in all the years before. The South Vietnamese army reeled under the attacks. Utter defeat was probably saved only by massive American air action. In May 1972 the United States mined the North's harbor at Haiphong and unleashed unparalleled bombing attacks on the North. A feature of these raids were new, highly accurate "smart" bombs.

As this was written, in August 1972, American policy under Mr. Nixon seemed to call for American air and naval support for the South Vietnamese into the indefinite future. We seemed to be embarked on a new effort to bomb the North Vietnamese to the conference table. (Actually negotiations to end the war began in 1968, but quickly turned into a propaganda forum with zero results.) There is more than a little evidence that not even the Russians and Red Chinese can get the North Vietnamese to either give up or ameliorate their terms for American surrender.

Under Mr. Nixon the character of the war has changed. It was still important to Americans to establish a non-Communist government in South Vietnam. But another issue entered the fray—American honor. The Nixon administration felt it could not and would not get out of Vietnam on any basis that could be construed as an American defeat. The Democratic party, under whose presidents the war had begun, came full circle and nominated Senator George McGovern of

South Dakota, who pledged to end all American involvement if elected.

The United States has made few greater mistakes in its history than its involvement in the war in Vietnam. Polls, articles, speeches too numerous to mention all overwhelmingly indicate American weariness and regretfulness over the war.

The gains have been small. South Vietnam remains a non-Communist nation, but there are grave doubts of the stability of its government or its permanence if American military aid were withdrawn. There are many who believe that if the latter occurred, South Vietnam would collapse very quickly or be overwhelmed militarily and politically by the North Vietnamese and Viet Cong. Even if this did not occur—or if American military involvement remained for years as a shield for South Vietnam—it faces horrendous problems. Much of its population has been uprooted and a great deal of its economy destroyed. Formerly an agrarian nation with a social structure tied to village life, South Vietnam has now been turned into an urban society with very little industry to support it. Under the most ideal circumstances, South Vietnam will be many years recovering from the war and re-establishing some workable social, economic, and political structure.

It can be argued, at least, that the United States has gained militarily from the war. The armed forces developed and tested a wide variety of sophisticated weapons and learned a number of new military techniques. Hundreds of thousands of troops became experienced in modern warfare. Segments of American industry associated with defense contracting made large profits from the war and developed manufacturing techniques.

In foreign affairs, the United States established its willingness to go to war for what it believed. Our commitments to allies and other nations were perhaps buttressed by the knowledge that American military might stood behind them. Conversely, Communists in developing nations may have discovered that insurgency could not be any more effective than armed invasion in taking over a non-Communist government, if the United States opposed it. Evidence that such a lesson has been learned perhaps lies in Chile, which voted a Marxist government into office through entirely constitutional means. Some observers feel this is the technique which Communist minorities will try to use in the future.

There are Americans, probably a significant majority, who believe the list of gains from the war is exceedingly small compared to the losses of the war. But other Americans will argue that the price of the war, admittedly high, must be paid by the United States to contain communism and to maintain America's place in the world.

The most obvious loss of the war is in terms of tens of thousands of American lives and hundreds of thousands of injured. When the casualties among the Vietnamese, Laotians, Cambodians, and Thais, as well as other nationalities, are included, it is a truly bloody war.

To reiterate a point made previously, the monetary cost of the war has been staggering in terms of dollars largely wasted in Vietnam that were desperately needed at home. The effect upon the American economy in inflation and unemployment has been significant.

The loss list must also include, again emphasizing a previous point, the great division which has occurred in America because of the war—the rioting and violence, the alienation of young people and others who opposed the war, the draft resistance in which hundreds of young Americans chose jail or exile rather than serve in the war.

The famed "credibility gap" is a product of the war. The American people were treated, particularly in the Johnson and Nixon administrations, to many encouraging reports on how well the war was going and how soon the enemy would be defeated, only to have these reports smashed by a new enemy offensive, a request for more troops, stepped-up American bombing, or the collapse of a South Vietnamese military effort.

Worse were the Pentagon Papers. These revealed that from 1964 through 1968, at least, American officials of the highest rank were plotting the war, thwarting efforts for a peaceful settlement, persisting in war efforts long after they were known to be ineffective if not self-defeating, and all the while concealing vital facts from the people and Congress, if not engaging in downright deception and lies.

As a result of these and other disclosures, large numbers of Americans have lost faith in the wisdom, honesty, and believability of government officials. This is a development in American democratic government of the utmost importance and danger.

A companion problem has been the growth of presidential war powers. The entire Vietnam War was conducted by the White House and the Executive branch. More than a little deception was used to enlist the necessary monetary aid of Congress, which was clearly not informed of all that was going on. There is, as a result, considerable agitation in Congress and among the people to curb presidential war powers so that Congress and the people may be consulted on war policies and be informed of the reasons for military actions.

Americans have undergone a truly traumatic experience with the war in discovering that our will and determination, let alone our military might, could not win.

In our past experience, we learned that all the United States had to do was enter a war, as in World Wars I and II and the Korean War, and our armies would be victorious. We never lost wars. As a matter of fact, experience had taught us that often all we had to do was rattle the sword, send a naval vessel, or at most land a few Marines on some foreign shore and we got our way. Even that much might not be necessary. Dispensing a few million dollars in American aid was frequently successful in achieving our ends.

But in Vietnam we found a nation that would not cower, would not be defeated by the military means we sought to apply, and would not negotiate. To the American mind, convinced of our own virtue, it was incredible, inconceivable intransigence. We found it extraordinarily difficult to believe that the North Vietnamese were sincere when they called Americans "aggressors," "imperialists," and "neo-colonialists" and swore to fight on until *we* gave up or were driven out.

After more than a quarter century of fighting in Vietnam, it must be concluded that the Communists of the North are sincere. Our failure to realize this follows Professor Stoessinger's thesis of the importance of imperception in the world. We saw the North Vietnamese as aggressors and they had the same view of us. If that had been correctly perceived years ago, instead of each labeling the other's views as insincere propaganda, a far different result might have been attained.

The persistence of the North Vietnamese and Viet Cong can perhaps be ascribed to other factors. The United States has had great difficulty understanding the Asian mind, and North Vietnam is a leading example. We cannot understand the attitude toward life and property, one being the willingness of Asians to sacrifice many lives for a cause and to attack or defend militarily against seemingly overwhelming odds. Another factor might be Robert Ardrey's idea from his book *The Territorial Imperative*.[4] He argues that many animals, including man, will defend their territory with great energy, even defeating or frightening off much more powerful attackers. It is to be presumed that Mr. Ardrey would consider Vietnam proof of his theory.

All of this has been traumatic for Americans—our failure to win, our long involvement in a hopeless war, the immorality of our military excesses in a frustrating search for victory, the violation of our sense of fair play by being cast into the role of bully, our fighting a courageous and determined adversary whom we would greatly admire if North Vietnam were fighting the Chinese or Russians, for example. Through this war, Americans have lost their sense of invincibility, self-righteousness, and morality—and none of it has been very easy to accept.

Of even greater importance for the subject of Soviet-American relations is the contention that our entire postwar foreign policies lie shattered in Vietnam. We listed four elements of this policy. These should be examined in the light of Vietnam.

Unrelenting enmity to communism. We have not even shown it in Vietnam, for we have at various times offered to include Communists in a coalition government in South Vietnam in return for an end to the war. While ordering the bombing of the North in 1972, President Nixon was visiting Peking and Moscow to reduce cold war tensions, curtail the arms race, and increase trade.

Our unrelenting enmity got us into Vietnam. It was the Truman Doctrine carried to its most illogical extreme. Under that doctrine we had to fight communism anywhere in the world, even when our national interests were only minimally involved. Later, efforts were made to develop explanations to make our vital interest seem more involved. One was the domino theory. If South Vietnam went Communist, all of Southeast Asia and eventually all of the Pacific would be lost.

The second explanation for our involvement was "honoring our commitments." If we did not, other nations of Asia would distrust us and seek succor from China and the Soviet Union. If ever valid, which many doubt, this reason was dissipated when America began its desperate efforts to extricate itself from the war.

Containment. The war in Vietnam hardly contained communism. It spread into the other nations of Southeast Asia. South Vietnam itself is not free of communism.

Military superiority. We most certainly had it in Vietnam, but it availed us very little. And, while we fought there, Soviet and Chinese military strength grew rapidly. The Soviets are nearing parity in atomic weapons, missiles, planes, and naval vessels. The Soviets are reported to be building their first aircraft carrier to beef up their already large fleet.

Willingness to use our military power to contain communism. We were certainly willing in Vietnam, but what did it achieve? At the same time we restrained the use of force in such places as the Congo, North Korea during the *Pueblo* crisis, the Israeli-Arab war, the India-Pakistan war. The results of restraint have been as desirable as the use of military force.

The question then is why did we use military force in Vietnam? The answer is rather simple. Our involvement in Vietnam dates back to 1950 and was greatly accelerated in the 1960s. Such actions were dictated by the old anti-Communist policies which originated under President Truman. The folly of Vietnam for the United States shattered those policies. The fact that a new Vietnam could probably not occur again today is striking evidence that new policies toward the Soviet Union have been and are being formulated.

Why did we persevere in these policies for so long, until they led to the tragedy of Vietnam? It is this question we must consider next.

15

A SEARCH
FOR CAUSES

THUS FAR OUR necessarily brief review of the history of Soviet-American relations has produced several causes or possible causes for the antagonism between the two countries, which has lasted more than half a century. These causes are worth enumerating.

1. The violent nature of the Russian Revolution with its godlessness and anti-property, totalitarian gospel, and the fear it caused among Americans.

2. The desire of the Soviets to export their revolution to America and other lands, and the fear and enmity it caused.

3. Imperceptions each nation had of the other, so that successive leaders of both consistently misinterpreted the intentions of the other.

4. The naïveté and relative inexperience of both

the Soviet and American leaders in the conduct of international affairs.

5. The inability of both nations to find ways to alter the pattern of mistrust, competition, and antagonism.

There are other causes of the cold war, however. They are in the areas of politics and economics and thereby would seem to have little to do with international relations. But they do. They may be among the more important causes for the cold war.

Politics can be one of man's highest callings, giving him the chance to lead his people and his nation, or it can be one of the lowest, a form of self-serving. Unfortunately the two are usually interwoven. To become a high-minded, altruistic politician, a person often must first engage in a good deal of self-service.

One other generality about politics seems in order. It is said that all men are motivated by money, power, or glory. Politicians may garner glory and sometimes some money, but I believe the most common lust of the man or woman in politics is power. They simply can't be very important in politics without at least a little of it. In the American context of politics, that power can be very great in an exceedingly small area— a precinct, ward, or county, a subcommittee of a state legislature or Congress, an area of expertise at the White House, a bureau or division in the vast federal bureaucracy. Space does not permit a digression into the workings of the American political system,[1] but consider only the power of city and county legislators in setting local property tax rates and determining how the money is spent.

Because of our insular nature, Americans tend to think of politics as an American phenomenon. Our particular style of it is different in many respects, but politics is a worldwide phenomenon. Every national leader is a politician. Hitler and Mussolini were. So was Stalin in his way and Khrushchev who followed him to power and Brezhnev, the Russian leader today. The political styles vary according to the individuals and their situations, but all have in common the need to maintain personal power through some form of politics.

The danger in politics (perhaps *evil* is not too strong a word) comes during that period when the politician is enlarging his popularity and power in pursuit of a higher level of leadership. The worldwide history of politics is studded with examples of politicians who have submerged wittingly or unwittingly the best interests of their people and their nation in the pursuit of personal power. Few would admit, even privately, that they deliberately did this, but such is the ability of human beings to rationalize and engage in intellectual dishonesty, that they do not find it difficult to convince themselves and thus their followers that their unwise and dangerous course is pure patriotism.

An example of this lies in Northern Ireland, where in the late 1960s and early 1970s violence and bloodshed have been rampant among Catholics and Protestants. The situation has been largely inexplicable to Americans. Even the British, who nominally rule Northern Ireland, do not profess to understand the continued, self-defeating radicalism and violence. The roots of the conflict are surely complex, going far into the past, fueled by current mistakes, and self-generated by the continuing violence. But Northern Irish intellectuals of both religious persuasions have explained to me in private conversations that one of the roots of the disorders is the simple fact that generations of Northern Irish politicians have exploited the divisive issues for personal political gain. Because of their political rhetoric, virtually all moderation and compromise have been lost. Bitter seeds of violence have been sown.

I believe similar statements can be made about many if not all the world's problems. The disputes between India and Pakistan, Israel and the Arab nations, Rhodesia and its black majority, are difficult at best, but solutions have often been made more difficult because of extremist rhetoric from self-serving politicians. Reasonableness and compromise have been harder to find.

Soviet-American relations have been worsened by political self-serving. The Soviet Union first. Americans, I believe, persist in the naïve notion that a succession of Soviet leaders (or Mao in the People's Republic of China) are dictators and thereby not politicians. We think they are dictators who simply issue commands and enforce their execution by military and police state methods of terror, liquidation, and repression. It is simply not so. These Communist leaders have been forced to be politicians, as well.

Consider the most absolute of modern dictators, Adolf Hitler. Despotic he surely was. He had a vast police apparatus to support him. But the secret of Hitler's messianic power over the German people was his assiduous tending to politics. Americans could not conceive of it, but Hitler had a magnetic personality and was a spell-binding orator. He gave voice and actions to German aspirations. He tended to politics through a massive propaganda campaign. In short, he formed a political base which lasted throughout the disastrous war.

Lenin, Stalin, Khrushchev, and Brezhnev have done no differently. Through speeches, propaganda, and other manifestations of politics, they rallied the Soviet people to make great sacrifices. Capitalists, Americans, Chinese, and others have been made enemies as national policy demanded. The whole secret society of the Soviets may be viewed as one gigantic political maneuver to create a popular following for Kremlin policies. Police-state methods have been used, to be sure, but largely against the recalcitrant and intellectuals.

Anti-Americanism has been the basis of the political effort in both the Soviet Union and China. By creating a capitalist, imperialist, warmongering enemy in America, the Russian and Chinese people have been kept on a more or less war footing, acquiescing in sacrifice,

paying for armament, serving in military forces, obey-
ing the edicts of the leaders rather than questioning
them or disobeying them. The Soviet Union is an immense amalgam of many nationalities and languages.
Uniting it is extraordinarily difficult. The Ukrainians
have long had separatist tendencies. How better to
unite them than through an appeal to nationalism because of the dangers inherent in the aggressive Americans. Politics, pure politics.

Has it been different in America? The United States
has had inspiring moments in which politicians sacrificed themselves for the public good. The late President Kennedy's best-selling book *Profiles in Courage*[2]
describes such incidents in the Senate. But we also
have a pronounced history of rabble-rousing for political gain. At various times politicians great and small
sought to turn prejudice into passion against the Irish,
Poles, Italians, and other ethnic groups, especially the
American Indian and the black. For over a century,
race-baiting was a device of white politicians, particularly in the South. In the opinion of more than a few,
the current issue over interracial school busing is the
same political maneuver in a new guise. Nor is this
technique a prerogative of any political spectrum.
Those of liberal persuasion have inflamed passions at
various times against businessmen, the less educated,
the wealthy, conservatives, and members of the military.

Since 1917 and the Bolshevik Revolution, the political path in America has been paved with anti-communism. A man or woman might be pro-labor, pro-business, black or racist, conservationist or apostle of economic growth, pro- or anti-intellectual, honest man or crook—and just about anything else—so long as his anti-communism was impeccable and secure. Illustrations of this statement could fill this book, but one will suffice. The labor movement, long containing avowed Socialists and not a few men with Communist leanings, made its gains in the 1930s and 1940s because it expunged all Communists and Socialists from its ranks.

The history of political anti-communism in America has been the subject of many books and needs to be treated only briefly here. There was no way that any man or woman urging moderation or compromise with the Soviets, let alone expressing avowed Communist or even Socialist doctrines, could be elected to public office in the United States.

A word has entered the American language as a result of all this—McCarthyism, for Senator Joseph R. McCarthy of Wisconsin.[3] The McCarthy era (roughly 1947 to 1957) is viewed by those who lived through it, either with loathing or, by his supporters, with embarrassment. Few any more think of him as a hero and patriot as some did in his heyday.

Historian Morison has called McCarthy "probably" a "plain rogue, who wanted the power to make Presidents and cabinet officials jump when he cracked the whip." Morison felt that McCarthy most likely had

his eye on the presidency. He described him as "satur-
nine, cruel, greedy," and said he "did nothing for the
people of his native state." Morison called him "one
of the most colossal liars in our history." [4]

McCarthy's favorite technique was to stand before
a wildly enthusiastic audience—or in the Senate where
he had immunity from libel suits—and wave a sheet of
paper on which he said were written the names of large
numbers of "card-carrying Communists" in the State
Department, military, the bureaucracy, Hollywood,
universities, or what have you. He promised never to
reveal the patriotic source for this vital information.
Nor did he reveal the names on his list. It is a simple
fact that not one Communist, near-Communist, fellow
traveler, red or pink was ever revealed, let alone convicted, on the basis of McCarthy's special information.

McCarthy was eventually censured by the Senate.
He had conducted his hearings into alleged Communist influence in America as virtual pogroms, with witnesses being subjected to unbelievable abuse with little,
if any, right of rebuttal. In the 1954 elections, he had
perpetrated one of the great out-and-out frauds of
American politics—a composite photo showing Mary-
land Senator Millard Tydings with Communist leader
Earl Browder. After his censure, McCarthy's power
waned and he died in 1957.

As Morison observes, "nobody who did not live
through" the McCarthy period "will ever believe what
a sound and fury [it] made up." Anti-communism ap-

proached witchhunt status. Simply trying to understand, let alone espousing the Communist viewpoint was grounds for investigation. Men and women who had flirted with and rejected communism in the 1930s were driven from public life. All dissent, on whatever subject, no matter how distant from Moscow and its ideology, was branded "red-lining." Loyalty to America became a fixation, with loyalty boards and loyalty oaths common. In the Eisenhower administration, over 6,900 "security risks" were purged in seventeen months. As Morison points out, "none . . . were really serious cases—mostly clerks who drank or talked too much or who had expensive girl friends." More importantly, some important career State Department officials were driven from office. The outcry even reached to the White House. Quite incredibly, even Truman and Acheson were branded as being "soft on communism." [5] There were trials of Communists and suspected Communists. A form of hysteria gripped the country. To dissent, let alone be Communist, was to be a handmaiden of Lucifer.

The cold war and anti-communism had a political usefulness in America other than advancing the notoriety of ambitious politicians. While we must refer to this in an American context and while the Soviet political system is radically different from ours, it must be suspected that at least some of the following is true in the USSR.

The most difficult political task in America is the

formation of a majority. The Founding Fathers were greatly concerned about a majority running roughshod over the rights of a minority and so wrote into the Constitution a system of checks and balances, separation of powers, and guarantees of individual liberty simply to make majority rule difficult. Over the years this initial difficulty was compounded by immigration and geography. Ours is a nation large in area with a big population fractionalized into many races, ethnic groups, religions, and economic classes. Freedom of expression guarantees the existence of radical, moderate, and conservative opinions on almost everything.

This diversity is reflected in the United States Congress, members of which represent individual states and districts. It is further reflected in the vast Washington bureaucracy, which is composed of departments, divisions, and bureaus regulating and representing special interests such as agriculture, labor, commerce, transportation, and so on.

The president, any president, is the person expected to find ways to amalgamate the nation's diversity into majority rule. He is the only person (the powers of the vice president being exceedingly small) voted on by all of the people. He is expected to form and maintain a popular majority among the people. Furthermore, he must find ways to command or persuade congressmen, bureaucrats, and lobbyists for special interest groups to carry out the policies he espouses.[6]

These are most difficult tasks and a succession of

modern presidents have struggled with them. They
have sought to develop policies and programs to unify
the diversity into a majority. There have been a number of unifying themes, but foremost among them
from 1947 to 1972 was anti-communism. Presidents
from Truman to Nixon, whose domestic policies were
often broadly criticized, were able to—or tried to—
earn popular support by citing the Communist menace
and the need for national defense, vigilance, and sacrifice. The succession of cold war crises and the danger
they seemed to pose for the nation have called forth
feelings of patriotism and desire to support the president in the nation's hour of need, even if he were disagreed with. Indeed, one of President Truman's accomplishments was the concept of a bipartisan foreign
policy, with the nation united in its opposition to communism and the Soviet Union.

This is not to suggest that there were not genuine
reasons for hostility toward communism or that the
Soviet Union is some lily-white innocent victim of the
American political process. But anti-communism has
had a certain political usefulness to presidents which
has been a factor in their maintenance of the Truman
foreign policies.

There is another, more human factor in the politics
of the cold war which a number of scholars are recognizing: the measurement of presidential greatness in
terms of crises. Modern historians and political scientists play an admitted game of ranking presidents as

great, near great, average, and poor. One of the criteria is the way the chief executive handled the crises of his administration. Rather obviously, to be accorded greatness the president must have had a serious crisis to deal with. Professor Clinton Rossiter, to name one, ascribes near-greatness to Theodore Roosevelt largely because his tenure lacked the major crises which marked the terms of Washington, Lincoln, Wilson, Franklin Roosevelt, and Truman.

A reaction has set in. Scholars are denouncing the equating of greatness with crises. Political Scientist Robert J. Bresler wrote in the August 17, 1970 issue of the *Nation*:

> Americans, especially liberals, should be embarrassed to recall, as Richard Neustadt, author of *Presidential Power,* has acknowledged, that they helped to create the myth which so loosely equated Presidential greatness with the exercise of war powers. . . . Great presidents would have to be strong presidents, and for liberals it was no more than coincidence that strong presidents invariably became war presidents.

Professor Hans J. Morgenthau, writing in the *New Republic* on June 14, 1969, confessed:

> I remember how I used to implore a succession of Presidents to assert their constitutional powers against Congress as long as I disagreed with the foreign policies to which Congress appeared to be committed. Yet, when I had given up on the potential for change

of the Eisenhower-Dulles foreign policies, I urged the Senate Foreign Relations Committee to establish itself as a kind of counter-Department of State. And, from 1965 onwards, I would have welcomed the influence the Congress, the Senate or, for that matter, any other agency of government could have exerted in order to change the course of American foreign policy.

Presidents are only human. It is only natural that they would seek greatness in their high office by being dynamic in dealing with the nation's crises. They were encouraged in this by scholars. They received further encouragement from the news media which give far more attention to action than inaction. President Kennedy received greater coverage for his blockade in the Cuban missile crisis than he would have had he opened negotiations. President Nixon received more newspaper space for sending American troops into Cambodia in 1970 than he did for not sending them into the Israeli-Arab or India-Pakistan conflicts. This is not to suggest that presidents have caused or prolonged cold war crises for reasons of personal publicity. But, again, the crises, once they occurred, added to their personal stature and encouraged an aura of dynamism and statesmanship.

The impasse in Soviet-American relations has also been of considerable short-range economic as well as political benefit to both nations. The Soviets used it to goad their people to high productivity and sacrifice. A foreign menace is a time-honored method for getting people to work more and expect less. The tremendous economic strides made by the USSR since World War II can only have been helped by the cold war competition in armaments and technology.

The United States has also achieved significant short-range gains. Since 1960 about 10 percent of our Gross National Product (the sum of all goods and services produced in the nation) has gone for defense. This spending has been a tremendous boon to defense-related industries. From 1962 through 1969, the top five defense contractors alone received over $50 billion from Uncle Sam. The top thirty contractors got over $133 billion.

Such colossal spending has benefited and thereby won the support of the military forces, the contractors who receive the money, the labor unions representing the workers in these industries, and entire communities where defense industries are located. Sizeable cities and even whole states—California being the leading example—depend in large measure on defense spending for their prosperity. Cuts in military appropriations—or failure to garner them in the first place—are highly sensitive politically. Indeed, were significant reductions to be made in armament spending without other government spending to offset it, the effect on the economy could be most damaging.

Both the American and Soviet economies depend—or at least they have ever since 1950—on a high level of government spending. Under cold war policies, much of this spending has gone for armaments.

But it must be pointed out that all this economic benefit from defense spending is detrimental in the long range. The huge sums the United States has poured into armaments have deprived the nation of vital funds for urban renewal, housing, education, mass transportation, pollution control, prison reform, health care, and many other civilian needs. We have chosen the cold war over social benefits.

The armament spending has also contributed to inflation, which plagued the nation during the Vietnam War. It is not a very large digression into economics to point out that armaments are relatively less productive to the economy than civilian goods. A tank is a tank and it costs whatever tanks cost. But a tank does not pull into the corner gas station or visit muffler shops, repair shops, have its wheels aligned, or stop for a quick wash. An automobile, to name one thing, does all these things. The investment in one automobile spins off into the entire economy, creating many jobs and producing much more money. The armaments contribute to inflation because they dump huge sums of tax money into the economy, but create relatively little ancillary labor.

However, more than the military-industrial complex has received an economic benefit from the cold war. The American space program, and presumably the Soviet too, has been accelerated by the cold war. Both nations were driven to develop a variety of spy and communication satellites for military purposes. The United States man on the moon program of the 1960s received many billions of tax dollars in part because it was conceived, in the press at least, as a space race with the Soviet Union. Americans were led to believe it would be some sort of national dishonor were a Russian to trod the moon ahead of an American. Lip-service was given to Soviet-American cooperation in space as a desirable goal, but it was not until President Nixon's visit to Moscow in 1972 that concrete steps were taken to achieve it.

Education was greatly enhanced financially by the cold war and its Soviet-American competition. Americans were shocked in 1957 when the Soviet Union launched the first earth satellite, Sputnik, ahead of the United States and alarmed when it remained ahead, launching bigger satellites and even men into orbit. Tax money was poured into the space program, but great sums also went into eradicating alleged deficiencies in the science programs of public schools. More money was suddenly available for teachers, labs, and textbooks.

Colleges, universities, and private companies received larger sums for research and development. Much of the money went for defense and space programs, but some was applied to pure research. So much money was spent in institutions of higher learning that men, such as economist John Kenneth Galbraith, expressed fears that universities and scientists were becoming dependent upon government financing and losing their independence.

Cold war tensions were translated into money in other ways. Consider what might be called the spying craze. From the 1950s into the 1970s, very large sums of money have been made out of our fascination with cold war spying. It is probably impossible to compute the amount of money made from books, movies, television programs, toys, and games with a spying motif.

The cold war created many jobs in private industry and in government. Immense profits were made from the tensions. And it is more than likely that the Soviet Union, despite its different economic system, also benefited from the cold war.

The political and economic factors discussed in this chapter are not the sole or even the major causes for the cold war and the persistent impasse and mistrust between the two nations. But they have had some effect.

16

THE NEW
REALITIES

A NEW AMERICAN policy toward the Soviet Union seems to be emerging in the 1970s. It is a policy based upon the realities of the world. We need to explore some of these.

Communism is simply not monolithic. The Russian brand of Marxism is not the only one in the world. There are many varieties—Chinese, Yugoslavian, Vietnamese, Chilean. Indeed, there are perhaps as many types as there are countries to practice it. Soviet leaders can no longer direct Communist ideology, nor can they fully control the domestic and foreign policies of their satellite nations without resorting to military force.

By the 1970s, communism was more characterized by nationalism than by Soviet orthodoxy. Each country seems to practice a brand of communism that differs in slight or large ways from the Soviet model, which is undergoing change itself.

The United States already has been forced to abandon its long-held belief and fear that identified the Communist menace with the Soviet Union. We have learned to conduct a variety of policies with Communist nations, virtually ignoring a nation such as Albania while developing relatively close economic and political ties with Yugoslavia. This breakdown in our belief in the monolithic nature of communism was symbolized by President Nixon's 1972 visit to the People's Republic of China and the improved relations it promised.

Another reality is that communism, as an ideology, is not the menace we believed for so long. Despite its great military strength, the Soviet Union possesses great weaknesses, particularly in agriculture. It must cope with growing dissent among artists, scientists, and intellectuals. The need is great for improved housing and other consumer goods. The Russian standard of living still lags behind that of the United States, Western Europe, and Japan.

Communism has been thoroughly rejected in Western Europe and in most of the rest of the world. Europe may be considered an example of why. The prosperity of Western Europe far exceeds that of Eastern Europe, whether under capitalist or Socialist economies. The degree of personal liberty in Western Europe contrasts sharply with that permitted in the East. There are people who will deliberately choose a Communist society over a Western one, but they are relative rarities. Across the world, democratic Japan serves as an example to Asians of the virtue of a non-Communist system.

Moreover, many nations have discovered that they can trade with the Soviet Union, accept its technical aid, and even buy military equipment from it, without being dragged into the Communist pit. Egypt and other Arab nations are outstanding examples, as are other nations of Africa and Asia, particularly India. Such nations have discovered that the two superpowers have not created an either-or situation in the world. They do not have to be dominated by either the Soviet Union or America. They can accept Communist aid and still retain their independence. Several nations, notably Indonesia, Ghana, and Egypt, which the United States had considered pulled into the Communist camp, later threw out Russian advisors and maintained their independence.

All of this has made it rather obvious that communism, as a worldwide doctrine of revolution, has lost its validity, if it ever had it. Even the Soviets give no more than lip-service to it. Various forms of capitalism and socialism have proven to be far more effective and appealing than the Soviet economic system. A less positive statement can be made about a democratic political system, but it has thrived in those lands where economic conditions, education, and past history make it feasible. There are simply too many nations of the world where chaotic conditions make a genuine democracy impractical.

The United States seems to be recognizing in the 1970s that communism and Soviet influence are not the original evils of the world. The American system, or at least one of the democratic systems, offers distinct advantages which the less developed nations are eager to enjoy. With the decline in our fears of the monolithic nature of communism and our discovery of its less than universal appeal, much of the ground on which anti-Communist battles have been fought for so long has fallen away.

Another reality is that the world is no longer divided into two camps. Particularly in the political seasons, the old rhetoric of dividing the world into "slave and free" or "communist and democratic" is heard. But the facts belie it. In economic terms, power in the world is now shared by the United States, the Soviet Union, Western Europe, and Japan. And such oil-rich peoples as the Arabs have found it relatively easy to drive hard bargains with much more powerful nations.

Nor is the world divided into halves politically. The People's Republic of China is generally being accorded superpower status, although a weak giant it is. No particular clairvoyance is needed to see further divisions of global power in the near future. Japan is simply too powerful economically to remain passive in world political affairs. Western Europe, particularly with the entry of Britain into the Common Market, should become a major factor in political decisions. In the more distant future South America and black African nations may well be able to combine to diffuse the political power of the Big Two. There is already talk and some effort to form the non-aligned nations, that is those neither in the Soviet or American camps, into a "third world." Perhaps, but the divisions between so many nations make it very difficult. It is more likely that several blocs such as those already mentioned will be formed.

The success of world recovery since 1945 and the growth of other power blocs have brought home to Americans in the 1970s the major reality that we can no longer dominate the world. We may be the most powerful nation in the world militarily and economically, but in Vietnam we learned that our power is relative and limited. We cannot do all. We cannot spread ourselves around the world in thousands of bases and fight a major war in Vietnam without suffering economic consequences. We do not have the resources. Too much needs to be done at home for Americans to become involved in civil squabbles somewhere else.

Nor is our limitation solely military and economic. Many of the nations of the world, probably most, simply do not want either American or Soviet meddling. Depending on their state of development, the nations want either aid or trade, but they demand their own destinies. Americans, I believe, are beginning to learn that they cannot force their system, methods, or will upon other nations. However painfully, we are learning and will have to learn still more that other peoples resent our intervention and feel quite capable of managing their own affairs.

The rhetoric denouncing such attitudes is the "new isolation." It equates an attitude recognizing American limitations, setting new domestic priorities, and allowing other nations to make their own choices with American withdrawal from world affairs in the 1920s and 1930s. There is a risk of such a return to isolationism, but there is no reason why the United States could not remain active in world affairs without trying to dominate the world.[1]

Still another reality is that the world's system of alliances, be they Russian- or American-inspired, are rather useless pieces of paper. An alliance is an agreement between nations that if one is attacked, the other will join in as an ally. The heyday of alliances was the nineteenth century when wars were gentlemanly. World Wars I and II were proof that alliances provoked war rather than kept the peace.

The basic problem with the alliance today is that in the nuclear age no nation will follow an ally into battle, no matter how friendly they might be. If the Soviet Union and the United States started slinging atomic missiles at each other, we may be certain that no European nation would join us in the hope it could be spared in the attack. America's postwar system of alliances may be useful in justifying our unilateral actions, such as in Vietnam, but as a means of keeping the peace they are not very valuable—as Vietnam attests. At least two of our allies in Vietnam—the Philippines and South Korea—were in effect paid by the United States to send troops.

Another very old approach to peace is the "balance of power" concept. Inimical nations will not attack each other, supposedly, if each knows the other has sufficient military strength to defeat it. President Nixon has been particularly enamored of this approach. He is using it in the Israeli-Arab, India-Pakistan conflicts, as well as between the United States and the Soviet Union.

Unfortunately, it too is historically less than promising. The balance of power did not prevent World War I. Nor was the 1967 Israeli-Arab war prevented. There is too much room for miscalculation. Political rhetoric can lead a nation to war for emotional reasons. Logic, on which the balance of power concept relies, is forgotten. No war, after all, is a product of reason.

The biggest problem with the balance of power approach is one of the major realities of the 1970s—the arms race. Both the United States and the Soviet Union are spending tens of billions of dollars a year on defense which they can ill afford, considering the domestic needs of both nations. When the arms purchases of the rest of the world, probably an incalculable sum, are added, the world's expenditures for armaments are alarming.

A minimal lesson of history, from ancient to current times, is that weapons have a way of being used, despite the best intentions not to. True, poison gases, first used in World War I, have not been used since, although there were a number of near misses in World War II. And nuclear weapons have not been exploded in combat since 1945. But the United States has dropped more bombs on Vietnam than were used in all of World War II. Ever more cunning weapons have been developed and used. Wars, large and small, have followed the possession of weapons.

One of the greatest legacies of the cold war and the anti-communism and anti-capitalism that fueled it has been the deeply held conviction in both the United States and the Soviet Union that each is a major military threat to the other and that the need for a strong defense takes precedence over all other concerns.

A further important reality of the 1970s is that the worldwide arms race is frightening, painfully expensive, and self-defeating.

These realities are being recognized in the 1970s, leading to new policies in America, the Soviet Union, and elsewhere in the world. By 1972, observers were already speaking of *détente,* a relaxing of world tensions. Despite the fighting in Southeast Asia, violence in the Middle East, and the India-Pakistan war over Bangladesh, there was an aura of hopefulness that a new era of international cooperation might be beginning.

One of the early signals of the new era was the speech by President Nixon on September 1, 1969 in Colorado Springs, Colorado, in which he announced his "strategy for peace." Almost immediately, the press dubbed it the "Nixon Doctrine." His strategy, he said, involved "maintaining defense forces strong enough to keep the peace—while not allowing wasteful expenditures to drain away resources we need for progress."

His strategy called for "limiting our commitments abroad to those we can prudently and realistically keep." Finally, his strategy called for "helping other free nations maintain their own security but not rushing in to do for them what they can and should do for themselves. It does not mean laying down our leadership. . . . It does mean forging a new . . . world stability in which the burden as well as the benefits are fully shared—a situation that does not rely on the strength of one nation but that draws strength from all nations."

The policy seemed to promise no more Vietnams by recognizing the limitations on American strength to be squandered abroad and the reality that other nations must share the tasks of keeping the peace.

Another important signal of the possibly new era was the *Ostpolitik* of Chancellor Willy Brandt of West Germany, for which he won the Nobel Peace Prize in 1971. Herr Brandt deliberately changed, sometimes reversing, his nation's foreign policies since World War II. He set out to repair West German relations with the

Soviet Union, Poland, East Germany, and other satellite countries. A series of agreements and treaties were signed in Moscow and other capitals.

The gist of these treaties was that West Germany, the most powerful nation in Europe economically, recognized the status quo that had developed following World War II. This meant accepting, however reluctantly, the loss of Silesia, Eastern Prussia, and other territories to Poland, the reality of a divided Germany, and German responsibility for World War II. The agreements called for renunciation of force between Germany and its neighbors to the east. Increased trade was provided for.

Brandt's *Ostpolitik* had several effects of importance. Tensions in Central Europe were greatly decreased. The Soviet Union and its satellites had long used West Germany as a whipping boy, citing its "menace" to justify various forms of repression and antipathy to the West. With the new treaties and acceptance of West Germany, this form of propaganda was no longer feasible. Too, West Germany took on a highly strategic role in Western Europe. It was still part of NATO and had strong ties with the United States, which continued to garrison troops there. But it had also opened a door to the East. It thus became a link across the Iron Curtain.

There were other developments in which Brandt had an important role. Talks were begun with East Germany to resolve the long-standing antipathy between the two halves of the former German nation.

Progress was slow, but by Brandt's renouncing the long-held West German intention to absorb East Germany into a unified nation, hopes developed that eventually the two Germanies could form some common bonds and a unified role in world affairs.

Ostpolitik also led to the signing of the Big Four agreement on Berlin on August 23, 1971. After prolonged negotiations, the United States, the Soviet Union, Britain, and France signed an agreement which went a long way toward defusing the Berlin issue, long a source of cold war crises. The Soviet Union agreed to share the responsibility with East Germany for the unimpeded access to Berlin which lies 110 miles inside East Germany. Other agreements were reached to ease travel by West Germans in East Germany. The close ties between West Germany and West Berlin were recognized. Later, West Berliners were granted privileges to visit with relatives in East Berlin through the infamous Berlin Wall.

Perhaps the greatest importance of Brandt's diplomatic activities was that it gave Brezhnev, Kosygin, and other Soviet leaders a chance to demonstrate to the United States and the rest of the world that they wanted a relaxation of world tensions, as well as increased trade with Western nations. Brezhnev showed considerable eagerness for an agreement in his dealings with Brandt. After the Treaty of Moscow was signed, he brought considerable pressure on the West German parliament to ratify it. Brandt shrewdly refused to submit it to the

Bundestag until the Big Four agreement on Berlin was reached. In these negotiations, the Soviets made several concessions of importance.

There is a question whether Brezhnev's actions signalled a new policy or whether the United States was simply giving new importance to signals they had previously ignored. Be that as it may, American diplomats began to react to the messages from Moscow. There were those in the United States who feared Brandt's policies. It was argued that the Soviet Union was merely repairing its fences in the West because of tensions along its four-thousand-mile border with China. Others maintained that Brezhnev was cleverly reaching for the old Soviet goal of undermining NATO and the defense of Western Europe. The expansion of Soviet influence into India, the growth of the Soviet navy and tensions in the Middle East were all cited as strange actions for a nation which sought *détente* with the United States. Clearly, the old mistrust of the USSR had not disappeared.

President Nixon took action on several diplomatic fronts. His initial thrust was to exploit the tensions between the Soviet Union and the People's Republic of China. The first American action was to sponsor in the fall of 1971 a resolution calling for the admission of Communist China into the United Nations. The United States had maneuvered for more than twenty years to keep the Mao government out of the UN General Assembly and Security Council. It was charged that American reversal of this policy was simple recognition that the Peking government was going to be admitted over American objections. The mainland government was quickly admitted, then the United States scored a defeat when the General Assembly voted to oust Nationalist China from the world body.

The bitterness of that defeat did not prevent Mr. Nixon from negotiating a visit to Peking in February 1972. The visit, as witnessed on television, was cordial. Thus far, little has come out of it in the form of agreements or treaties. But direct ties were forged between Washington and Peking, although no formal diplomatic recognition has been announced. But by his actions, Mr. Nixon ended the long isolation of the People's Republic from the rest of the world. The United States accepted the reality that the Peking government controlled the world's most populace nation. Hope for improved relations in the future was engendered.

Two other results may be of great importance ultimately. President Nixon's visit signaled American involvement in the frigid relations between the Soviet Union and the People's Republic of China. At this writing, no direction to this involvement has been revealed. But involved we are. The visit also caused a new direction in the foreign policy of the economic giant of the Far East, Japan. The Japanese, who had long hitched their wagon to the American star, were stunned by American overtures to Peking. Almost immediately, the Japanese began seeking a more inde-

pendent course, searching for increased trade and better relations with other nations of the world, including
the Republic of China. What will come of this is un-
predictable at this point, but clearly something of importance in world affairs could occur. President Nixon's
visit to Peking was followed by a visit to Moscow in
May 1972, the first ever by an American president. The
fact that the visit occurred at all was of significance.
Shortly before the journey was to take place, the North
Vietnamese launched a major offensive into South
Vietnam. It was immensely effective. To stem the tide
the United States resumed bombing of North Vietnam
and, as previously mentioned, it even mined the North
Vietnamese harbor at Haiphong.

In the not very distant past, such American actions
would have led to Soviet denunciations of the United
States and cancellation of the scheduled meetings. But
this did not occur and Mr. Nixon went to Moscow.
The sessions were businesslike and both Nixon and
Brezhnev worked mightily to produce a series of agreements. They agreed on cooperative exploration of
space. American and Soviet space ships are to rendez-
vous in orbit in 1975. Other agreements were reached
for pooling research and resources of both countries in
medical and environmental fields. Soviet scientists
will visit St. Louis, Missouri, to study air pollution and Lake Tahoe, Nevada, to investigate water
pollution. American scientists will perform similar
functions in Leningrad and Lake Baikal, USSR. Even-

tually, thirty such scientific exchanges will take place.

The most important agreement involved disarmament. Both nations, reacting to the folly of the arms race, had begun the so-called SALT (Strategic Arms Limitation Talks) talks two and a half years before. Part of the evidence of a thaw in cold war tensions was the efforts of both nations to soften their stands on armaments to reach agreement in those talks. Nixon and Brezhnev signed an agreement that was the fruition of those discussions. The agreement is a first step toward disarmament.

In the agreement each nation promised to limit its deployment of Anti-Ballistic Missiles (ABM) to two installations, one protecting the national capital and one guarding a major offensive missile site. The agreement recognizes the realities that full deployment of ABMs would be extremely expensive and that the missiles are of dubious effectiveness.

The two leaders agreed to freeze each nation's stockpile of offensive, land-based missiles at the present level: 1,618 for the Soviet Union to 1,054 for the United States. Submarines carrying nuclear missiles will be frozen also under the agreement at 42 for the USSR and 41 for the United States. Some shifting in the mix of land and sea missiles was permitted.

The agreement does not offer the parity between the two nations its language would seem to indicate. Nothing was said about the type of warheads carried by the missiles. This leaves the United States far ahead, for it has developed the so-called MIRV system by which multiple nuclear warheads can be fired by a single rocket. Thus, the United States has 5,700 warheads to 2,500 for the Soviets, who have yet to develop the MIRV system. Nor does the agreement prevent either nation from developing more powerful or more accurate bombs and missiles. About all it accomplishes is to change the arms race from an exercise in quantity to one seeking quality.

Nixon and Brezhnev did agree to continue the SALT talks, offering at least hope that some further disarmament agreements can be reached in the future. Nevertheless, the arms race remains a paramount issue between the two superpowers.

Almost immediately upon his return from Moscow and his announcement of the arms limitation agreement, Mr. Nixon and his secretary of defense, Melvin Laird, announced plans to spend several billion dollars for a new round of offensive weapons. This became an issue in the 1972 political campaign. Senator McGovern, the Democratic nominee, announced his plans to cut defense spending by $30 billion a year without harming the nation's defense capabilities. Upon being renominated for president, Mr. Nixon's first action was to address the American Legion convention in Chicago and state that such cuts would make the United States a second-rank military power to the Soviet Union and put the nation in an inferior position in negotiations with the Russians. A major political issue was thus joined.

National defense is a highly emotional issue in the United States and presumably in the Soviet Union. It leads to immediate use of scare tactics that unilateral disarmament will lead to quick invasion and subjugation. Senator Henry Jackson of the State of Washington ran for the Democratic nomination for president urging even greater expenditures for armaments. To many Americans it is simple common sense that a strong defense leads to security, even though the history of the world demonstrates that armaments lead to wars, not security.[2] The world's approach to disarmament for the last half century and longer has been to negotiate collective disarmament agreements, which have proven to be very difficult to negotiate and harder to enforce.

Yet the world's expenditures for armaments are intolerable. They seem to benefit only a small group of manufacturers and dealers in weapons, along with the military leaders whose careers are enhanced by large standing military forces. In the United States, these elements seem able to mount a high level of rhetoric which equates defense spending with patriotism, Mom, God, and all that is valuable in life. As a result, public attitudes in America are clearly in favor of ever more powerful defense spending.

The result ever since 1950 has been recurrent rounds of offensive-defensive weaponry. Both the

United States and the Soviet Union possess weapons capable of destroying each other and the entire planet several times over. Defense spending in both nations is a classic case of overkill fed by fear.

President Nixon's trip to Moscow appears to have had effects in at least two other areas, trade and Vietnam. Considerable efforts have been made to increase trade. An agreement has been signed under which the United States will sell a large amount of grain to the Soviet Union. This agreement has become a political as well as an economic issue, with repercussions from the less powerful grain dealers and threats to increase the price of bread to consumers. The USSR indicates it would like to have the latest American electronic and other technical gear. The United States is in need of various ores from the Soviet Union. American industrialists have been negotiating to open factories in the Communist nation. Difficulties have been encountered in amalgamating the two economic systems. But in 1972, as this was written, there was at least a beginning of increased trade between the two nations.

The fact that the USSR has indicated it wants the trade is of great importance, for it is a tacit admission of weakness on the part of the Soviet Union. They obviously need grain and technical devices. The new Soviet leaders are willing to admit the realities of their existence, something that simply would not have occurred in the Stalin era. Because of that, the potentials for a lessening of cold war tensions are immense.

It has also become clear that Mr. Nixon discussed the Vietnam War with Soviet leaders while in Moscow. There is considerable evidence that the Soviet desire for trade was used as bait to get Brezhnev to try to persuade the North Vietnamese to come to a negotiated settlement of the war. Near the end of October 1972 (shortly before the presidential election), Henry Kissinger, President Nixon's advisor, announced that the general terms for ending the war had been reached with North Vietnam. The terms are a ceasefire in place in South Vietnam; total withdrawal of all U.S. and Allied troops; cessation of the introduction of new weapons into the country; formation of a new government in Saigon after "free and democratic" elections held under international supervision; exchange of prisoners; stopping of military activity in Cambodia and Laos; reunification of all Vietnam "step by step through peaceful means"; and American aid to reconstruct North Vietnam. By mid-December the agreement had not been signed, however, and fighting and bombing continued unabated.

The policies of Mr. Nixon and Mr. Brezhnev are too new for accurate assessment. But it may safely be said that in the early 1970s the two nations were recognizing the new realities of the world and searching for fresh accommodations. At the same time old ideas based on mistrust were lingering on. There was surely as much opportunity for misunderstanding as for accommodation.

A reality in the United States is the eighteen-year-old vote. Young people have a chance in the years ahead to drastically affect the old futile struggle between the Soviet Union and the United States. Much of the fifty-year struggle between the two nations is now ancient history to them. Indeed, today's revolutionaries are rejecting communism as too conservative.

There are ample opportunities for the young people of the world to seek cooperation—in space, pollution, trade, education, health, mass transportation, and many other problems. By concentrating on these mutual problems, the two governments can perhaps discover the trust that will break down historic political suspicions.

A start must be made somewhere. For fifty-five years —one-fourth of America's history—we have engaged in militant, virile anti-communism. Whatever it may be said to have accomplished in the past, it has now reached the point of being self-defeating and exceedingly dangerous for the world.

Young people are now the dominant age group in the world. They do not come automatically equipped with the virulent anti-communism of the past. They are not prisoners of past attitudes and mistakes. They have an unparalleled opportunity, as their generation moves toward the seats of national power, to shake off past attitudes and approach the problems of peace with new ideas.

NOTES

Chapter 1

1. Figures computed from statistics supplied by the U.S. Arms Control and Disarmament Agency as reported in *The New York Times Encyclopedic Almanac,* 1971, p. 720. The figures are said to include the "military activities of Department of Defense, military assistance, atomic energy programs, and defense-related activities of civilian agencies" and "space research and technology."

2. Report of the Subcommittee on United States Security Agreements and Commitments Abroad of the Senate Foreign Relations Committee, December 1970, better known as the Symington Report. Available from the Government Printing Office in Washington.

3. Background Material Foreign Assistance Programs, 92nd Congress, 1st Session.

4. The full list of agencies is illuminating: American Battle Monuments Commission, Agency for International Development, Agriculture Department, Atomic Energy Commission, Bureau of Narcotics and Dangerous Drugs, Central Intelligence Agency, Commerce Department, Customs Department, Defense Department, Environmental Science Services Administration, Export-Import Bank, Federal Aviation Administration, Federal Bureau of Investigation, Foreign Agriculture Service, General Services Administration, Health, Education and Welfare Department, Housing and Urban Development Department, Immigration and Naturalization Service, Interior Department, Internal Revenue Service, Justice Department, Labor Department, Maritime Administration, National Aeronautics and Space Administration, National Science Foundation, Peace Corps, Public Health Service, Smithsonian Institution, State Department, Tennessee Valley Authority, Transportation Department,

Treasury Department, United States Information Agency, United States Travel Service, Veterans Administration. This list was compiled in January 1971 by *The New York Times.* It reported that each of these agencies maintains personnel attached to American embassies abroad "reporting through separate channels to different department heads who compete with the Washington bureaucracy for the ear of the White House."

5. *Nations in Darkness: China, Russia and America* by John G. Stoessinger, Random House, New York, 1971.

6. I am indebted to Professor Stoessinger's theory that the USSR and the United States were guilty of imperception of each other, but I have greatly expanded his concept and thereby assume responsibility for it.

Chapter 2

1. *Woodrow Wilson, Life and Letters* by Ray Stannard Baker, Vol. VII, p. 350, Doubleday, Doran & Co., New York, 1939.

2. *Russia and the West Under Lenin and Stalin* by George F. Kennan, p. 19, Little Brown & Co., Boston and Toronto, 1960, 1961.

3. *American Russian Relations, 1781–1947* by William Appleman Williams, Rinehart & Co., New York and Toronto, 1952.

4. *Elihu Root* by Philip C. Jessup, p. 361, Dodd Mead, New York, 1938.

5. Williams, p. 87.

6. Quoted by Williams, p. 93.

7. Quoted by Williams, p. 92.

8. Stoessinger, p. 116.

9. *Pravda,* Sept. 15, 1957.

10. *The Public Papers of Woodrow Wilson, 1917–1924* by

R. S. Baker and W. E. Dodd, Vol. II, p. 70, Harcourt, Brace, New York, 1927.

11. *The Oxford History of the American People* by Samuel Eliot Morison, p. 883, Oxford University Press, New York, 1965.

12. Quoted in *The Road to Teheran* by Foster R. Dulles, p. 164, Princeton University Press, Princeton, N. J.

13. Quoted in *Radicalism in America* by Sidney Lens, p. 280, Thomas Y. Crowell Co., New York, 1966.

14. Quoted in Lens, p. 280.

Chapter 3

1. *Izvestia,* March 28, 1917. Quoted in *Soviet Politics At Home and Abroad* by Frederick L. Schuman, p. 169, Alfred A. Knopf, New York, 1946.

2. *Pravda,* November 19, 1917. Quoted in Schuman, pp. 169–70.

3. All quotes from Schuman, pp. 171–2.

4. *Mein Leben* by Leon Trotsky, p. 259, S. Fischer Verlag, Berlin, 1930.

5. *Understanding the Russians* by Foy D. Kohler, p. 45, Harper & Row, New York, 1970.

6. *Sochineniya* (Complete Works) of V. I. Lenin, Fourth edition, Vol. XXVII, p. 553, State Publishing House for Political Literature, Moscow, 1950.

7. *Current Digest of the Soviet Press,* January 4, 1961, p. 4. Quoted in *Soviet Foreign Propaganda* by Frederick C. Barghoorn, p. 42, Princeton University Press, Princeton, New Jersey, 1964.

8. *Voprosy Ideologicheskol Raboty,* pp. 278–9. Quoted in Barghoorn, pp. 52–3.

9. Lens, *op. cit.,* p. 187.

10. For a fuller account of this labor turmoil read the author's

Dissent in America, Chapters 2 and 3, McGraw-Hill Book Co., New York, 1971.

11. The 1920s were a particular time of hate campaigns against minorities in the United States. Anti-Semitism appeared openly for the first time, nourished significantly by Henry Ford. Several notorious anti-Catholic pamphlets were circulated. Anti-Negro campaigns were at their zenith. The Ku Klux Klan reached the peak of its power, North and South. Lynchings were common. The year 1919 was the worst single year for race riots in our history. Thus, anticommunism was only *one* of the sources of hate. The reasons for this season of prejudice ought to be a subject for scholarly study.

12. Stoessinger, p. 129.

Chapter 4

1. U. S. Congress, Senate, *Congressional Record,* 66th Congress, Second Session, April 28, 1920, p. 6208.

2. *Saturday Evening Post,* April 30, 1921.

3. ARA *Bulletin,* Number 41, October 1923, pp. 2–3.

4. *The New York Times,* January 17, 1931.

5. Quoted in *Americans and the Soviet Experience, 1917–1933* by Peter G. Filene, p. 87, Harvard University Press, Cambridge, Mass., 1967.

6. Schuman, pp. 274–5.

7. Both quoted in Schuman, p. 283.

Chapter 5

1. Schuman, p. 365.

2. *America and Russia in a Changing World* by W. Averell Harriman, p. 12, Doubleday and Co., Garden City, N. Y., 1970.

3. Schuman, pp. 374–5.

4. Both quoted in Harriman, p. 12.

5. These are the Soviet figures printed in *Pravda* on June 11, 1944. Quoted in *Soviet Foreign Policy During the Patriotic War: Documents and Materials II,* p. 87, London, 1945.

6. Harriman, pp. 18–19.

7. Harriman, p. 26.

Chapter 6

1. Quoted in *The Last 100 Days* by John Toland, p. 113, Random House, New York, 1965, 1966.

2. Toland, p. 113.

3. Toland, p. 91.

4. In his book, previously cited, Harriman mentioned the difficulty the "meaning of words" posed in American relations with Russia. ". . . to us a 'friendly neighbor' meant a country with which we did not have undue trouble, while to Stalin a 'friendly neighbor' meant a country which he dominated and controlled," p. 34.

5. *The Rivals: America and Russia Since World War II* by Adam B. Ulam, p. 15, Viking Press, New York, 1971.

Chapter 7

1. For a detailed analysis of the United States as a government of special interests, see the author's *The American Political System,* Parents' Magazine Press, New York, 1972.

2. *Stalin and His Generals* by Seweryn Bialer, p. 614, Pegasus, New York, 1969.

3. Eisenhower apparently believed a gigantic Nazi hoax that a nearly impregnable fortress had been built in Bavaria for a last, fight-to-the-death stand by Hitler. Eisenhower sent a lot of American troops southward to thwart Hitler's purpose. No such fortress existed and the troops were wasted. Such are the fortunes of war.

4. The uprisings against the tsars in 1905; the Kerensky revolution in February 1917; and the Bolshevik Revolution in October of the same year.

5. Harriman, p. 33.

6. Quoted in Toland, p. 46.

7. The Big Three cast had changed by the time of the Potsdam meeting. Stalin was still there, but Roosevelt was dead, replaced by Truman. He was new to his tasks and far from confident in his role as world leader. Churchill had lost the British elections. The prime minister was now Clement Attlee. Both Truman and Attlee, lacking the charisma of Roosevelt and Churchill, seemed inferior substitutes at the time. History gives a different accounting, however.

8. Read *The Fall of Japan* by William Craig, Dial Press, New York, 1967.

9. The most celebrated advocate of such policies in the immediate postwar era was Henry Wallace, secretary of agriculture in Truman's administration. Wallace was branded a radical and Communist sympathizer, resigned from the cabinet and, in 1948, unsuccessfully ran for president on the far-left Progressive party ticket. Prior to the Truman presidency, Wallace had been a highly regarded secretary of agriculture for Roosevelt and the Vice President in 1941–45. Roosevelt dumped Wallace as a running mate in 1944 and chose Truman. Historians have not ceased to speculate on how the world might have changed had Roosevelt kept Wallace in 1944, thus making him president instead of Truman in 1945.

Chapter 8

1. The term "cold war" to describe the frigid relations between the U. S. and the USSR is believed to have been used first by columnist Walter Lippmann in a series of newspaper articles. The equally popular term "Iron Curtain" to describe the Soviet sphere of influence in Eastern Europe was coined by Winston Churchill in a speech in Fulton, Mis-

souri, on March 5, 1946. He said that "from Stettin in the Baltic to Trieste in the Adriatic, an iron curtain has descended across the continent" behind which "police governments" rule Eastern Europe. He went on to suggest that the Russians did not want war, but "they desire . . . the fruits of war and the indefinite expansion of their power and doctrines." The speech, coming from so respected a man as Churchill, had an immense effect on American public opinion and policies.

2. *Present At the Creation* by Dean Acheson, p. 221, W. W. Norton & Co., New York, 1969.

3. Careful reading of Acheson does not make it clear whether his "chief" is Truman or General George C. Marshall, the secretary of state.

4. Nurture is a strange and probably unfortunate choice of words by Acheson, normally a most careful writer. To nurture is by definition "the act or process of raising or promoting the development of" something. It is unlikely that Acheson means he *promoted* the crisis for a week. Presumably he was trying to resolve it.

5. Acheson, p. 219.

6. *Intervention and Revolution* by Richard J. Barnet, p. 121, New American Library, New York, 1968.

7. As quoted by Acheson, p. 222.

8. *A New Foreign Policy for the United States* by Hans J. Morgenthau, p. 17, Frederick A. Praeger, New York. Copyright 1969 by the Council on Foreign Relations, Inc.

9. Morgenthau, p. 17.

10. Morgenthau, p. 18.

Chapter 9

1. Quoted in Acheson, p. 228.

2. Quoted in Acheson, p. 233.

3. Quoted in Acheson, p. 234. Acheson was somewhat cynical in referring to the Marshall speech. "If General Marshall believed, which I am sure he did not, that the American people would be moved to so great an effort as he contemplated by as Platonic a purpose as combating 'hunger, poverty, desperation, and chaos,' he was mistaken. But he was wholly right in stating this as the American *governmental* purpose," p. 233.

4. Indeed, when one travels in Western Europe, as I have extensively, the continuation of military and economic aid to such wealthy countries seems unnecessary, to make an understatement. Large contingents of American troops, for example, are quartered in West Germany, one of the most economically prosperous nations in the world.

5. *America and the Cold War* by Richard J. Walton, pp. 41–2, Seabury Press, New York, 1969.

6. Acheson, pp. 234–5.

7. Ulam, pp. 129–30.

8. Historian Samuel Eliot Morison of Harvard writes in his *Oxford History, op. cit.,* that the United States "offered" the Soviet Union the same benefits of the Marshall plan.

9. For one, Morison, p. 1057.

10. There were rebellions in Hungary, Poland, and Czechoslovakia, put down by the Red Army. But there is little evidence that Western Europe instigated them. Yugoslavia, of course, pursues an independent Communist line, and Rumania maintains an element of independence in foreign affairs. Albania is hostile to the Soviet Union and is in the Chinese Communist sphere. Again, it is difficult to blame the West for these developments. Without doubt Western Europe has been a magnet for Eastern Europeans. But this did not lead to a Soviet attack. The result was extreme security measures, symbolized by the wall separating East and West Berlin.

11. Correctly the European Economic Community. Originally

six members—France, Italy, West Germany, Belgium, The Netherlands, Luxembourg—it has become nine with the addition of Denmark, Britain, and Ireland.

Chapter 10

1. Washington's Farewell Address, delivered September 17, 1796.

2. Quoted by Walton, p. 61.

3. For these analyses of Soviet thinking I am indebted to Ulam, p. 170.

4. Ulam, p. 172.

5. Ulam, p. 172.

6. For example, one of the most vehement critics of the war in Vietnam, Dr. Benjamin Spock, has repeatedly said he supported the Korean War.

7. General MacArthur did not believe the Soviet Union would enter the war he envisioned. Truman at the time and most of the analysts since believed the real danger was the United States getting involved in a massive land war in Asia. We were not prepared to fight it or to make the sacrifices required.

Chapter 11

1. Ulam's description of the plan. It is hard to realize how the scheme could work, even if it had been put into effect, for it omits the outstanding quality of the Germans, a quality which makes them feared to this day—their energy. It is said 80 percent of the German nation arises at 6 A.M. Considering the amazing postwar recovery of Germany—it is the leading industrial power of Europe and an economic competitor of the United States—perhaps they arise even earlier.

2. Lawrence W. Martin, "The American Decision to Rearm Germany" in *American Civil-Military Decisions*, Harold

Stein, editor, pp. 648–9, University of Alabama Press, Birmingham, 1963.

3. From a statement on October 21, 1950, to the foreign ministers of the USSR and its Eastern European satellites.

4. *Ibid.*

5. Stoessinger, pp. 154–5. His inside quotes are from *The New York Times* of April 3–4, 1954.

6. State Department Press Release, November 16, 1954.

7. Stoessinger, pp. 157–8.

Chapter 12

1. The word originated in an article by Dulles in *Life* magazine in January 1956. Dulles wrote: "The ability to get to the verge without getting into the war is the necessary art. If you cannot master it, you inevitably get into war. If you try to run away from it, if you are scared to go to the brink, you are lost. . . . We walked to the brink and we looked it in the face. We took strong action."

2. In one memorable incident, "K"—as he was invariably dubbed in the American press—lauded American breakfast cereals and urged their production in the USSR. Years later, United States government reports found most of the cereals to be of very little value nutritionally.

3. Adding a new word to the language, "summitry."

Chapter 13

1. *The President as World Leader* by Sidney Warren, p. 393, McGraw-Hill Book Co., paperback edition, New York, 1964.

2. *Cold War and Counterrevolution: The Foreign Policy of John F. Kennedy,* by Richard J. Walton, p. 141, Viking Press, New York, 1972.

Chapter 14

1. Among the better accounts are Hal Dareff's *The Story of*

Vietnam (revised edition) and the same author's *From Vietnam to Cambodia,* Parents' Magazine Press, New York, 1971.

2. It has been contended by some of those who were close to Kennedy that he had decided prior to his death to end American involvement in the war if he was reelected.

3. This was a 43-volume history of the war prepared in 1968 by the Department of Defense. Classified "top secret," the report was purloined, photocopied, and distributed to various newspapers, which published excerpts from them in June 1971.

4. Atheneum, New York, 1966.

Chapter 15

1. Read the author's *The American Political System, op. cit.*

2. Harper and Row, New York, 1964.

3. He is hardly the only one. Representative Martin Dies of Texas, long-time head of the House Un-American Activities Committee, is a close rival as a "Red baiter." Had it not been for the greater notoriety of McCarthy, Dies might hold first rank among anti-Communists. More to the point, President Truman, in his *Memoirs,* called the infamous House committee "the most un-American thing in America in its day."

4. *Oxford History,* p. 1075. As evidence of the liar charge, Morison, who is basically a military historian, pointed out that during the war McCarthy had been an air combat intelligence officer in the Marines 4th Air Wing. While campaigning he claimed to have flown countless air missions as a tail gunner, killing thousands of the enemy. McCarthy's discharge rank of captain would have made him the war's highest ranking tail gunner, invariably an enlisted man's position.

5. To my knowledge, President Nixon has not stated whether he feels pride or remorse in his early career as a militant anti-Communist. He was elected to both the House and

Senate through use of the "soft on communism" charge against his opponents. As a member of the House Un-American Activities Committee he earned a reputation as a militant anti-Communist in part through his arranging the confrontation between Alger Hiss, a former State Department official, and writer-editor Whittaker Chambers, who accused Hiss of turning secrets over to him, an avowed Communist at the time. Hiss was convicted of perjury in two of the more famous trials in American history. Nixon's reputation led to his election as vice president under Eisenhower in 1952 and 1956. Whatever else might be said, Mr. Nixon's career illustrates how anti-communism was used in the postwar era as a stepping stone to political power. Political memories are long. In the 1972 campaign, Mr. Nixon's early career was still being used against him by his opponent for president, George McGovern. That is perhaps as good an illustration as any of changing political attitudes toward communism.

6. I have discussed these matters previously in my book *Presidential Power: How Much Is Too Much?*, McGraw-Hill Book Co., New York, 1971.

Chapter 16

1. Europeans know this much more than Americans. I've heard ordinary, not particularly well-informed Europeans say that the United States must learn that it cannot dominate the world as France, Germany, and Britain learned it after so much travail.

2. Two points need to be made here. One is that the American people have not felt any more secure with their strong military possessions since 1950 than they did when the nation disarmed following all its previous wars. Second, a number of nations, almost totally disarmed, have managed to live in peace and relative security with belligerent neighbors. The outstanding example is the Arab kingdom of Kuwait. Tiny, but fabulously rich in oil, it is coveted by its larger neighbors. Yet Kuwait has managed to remain independent and unthreatened with no more than a minimal police force.

SELECTED READINGS

Acheson, Dean: *Present At the Creation: My Years in the State Department;* W. W. Norton, New York, 1969.

Barghoorn, Frederick C.: *Soviet Foreign Propaganda;* Princeton University Press, Princeton, New Jersey, 1964.

Bennett, Edward M.: *Recognition of Russia;* Blaisdell, Waltham, Massachusetts, 1970.

Dallin, David J.: *Soviet Foreign Policy After Stalin;* J. B. Lippincott, New York, 1960.

Fulbright, J. William: *The Arrogance of Power;* Random House, New York, 1966.

Griffith, William F.: *Cold War and Coexistence;* Prentice-Hall, Englewood Cliffs, New Jersey, 1971.

Harriman, W. Averell: *America and Russia in a Changing World;* Doubleday, Garden City, New York, 1971.

Kennan, George F.: *Russia and the West Under Lenin and Stalin;* Little, Brown, Boston, 1960, 1961.

Kissinger, Henry A.: *The Necessity of Choice: Prospects of American Foreign Policy;* Harper, New York, 1960, 1961.

274

Kohler, Foy D.: *Understanding the Russians;* Harper, New York, 1970.

Lasky, Victor: *The Ugly Russian;* Trident, New York, 1965.

Liston, Robert A.: *The American Political System,* Parents' Magazine Press, New York, 1972.

Liston, Robert A.: *Presidential Power: How Much Is Too Much?;* McGraw-Hill, New York, 1971.

Morgenthau, Hans J.: *A New Foreign Policy for the United States;* Praeger, New York, 1969.

Overstreet, Harry and Bonaro: *The Strange Tactics of Extremism;* W. W. Norton, New York, 1964.

Schuman, Frederick L.: *Soviet Politics At Home and Abroad;* Alfred A. Knopf, New York, 1946.

Sherwin, Mark: *The Extremists;* St. Martin's Press, New York, 1963.

Stoessinger, John G.: *Nations in Darkness: China, Russia and America;* Random House, New York, 1971.

Toland, John: *The Last 100 Days;* Random House, New York, 1965, 1966.

Ulam, Adam B.: *The Rivals: America and Russia Since World War II;* Viking, New York, 1971.

Walker, Brooks R.: *The Christian Fright Peddlers;* Doubleday, Garden City, New York, 1964.

Walton, Richard J.: *America and the Cold War;* Seabury, New York, 1969.

Walton, Richard J.: *Cold War and Counterrevolution: The Foreign Policy of John F. Kennedy;* Viking, New York, 1972.

Williams, William Appleman: *American Russian Relations 1781–1947;* Rinehart, New York, 1952.

INDEX